Stories of Pain, Trauma and Survival
A Social Worker's Experiences and Insights from the Field

Sarah E. Meisinger

NASW PRESS

National Association of Social Workers
Washington, DC
James J. Kelly, PhD, ACSW, LCSW, *President*
Elizabeth J. Clark, PhD, ACSW, MPH, *Executive Director*

First impression July 2009
Second impression March 2011

Cheryl Y. Bradley, *Publisher*
Lisa M. O'Hearn, *Managing Editor*
Dac Nelson, *Copyeditor*
Linda Elliott, *Proofreader*
Tom Fish, *Indexer*

Cover by Eye to Eye Designs
Interior Design by Electronic Quill Publishing Services
Printed and bound by Balmar

Library of Congress Cataloging-in-Publication Data

Meisinger, Sarah E.
Stories of pain, trauma, and survival: a social worker's experiences and insights from the field / by Sarah E. Meisinger. — 1st ed.
    p. cm.
Includes bibliographical references and index.
ISBN 978-0-87101-391-0 (alk. paper)
1. Social workers. I. Title.
HV40.35.M45 2009
361.3—dc22

Printed in the United States of America

Table of Contents

About the Author

Sarah E. Meisinger, MSW, LICSW, is a clinical social worker currently in practice in central Minnesota. Her social work experience includes work with nonprofit agencies, child welfare services, and veterans' health care. She is an adjunct faculty member with St. Cloud State University's Social Work Department.

Introduction

I was driving home from an especially hard day and I remember thinking, as I frequently have, "Why am I doing this work?" I was mentally and emotionally exhausted and I was unsure how I'd find the energy to return to my office the following day. I drove into the garage, turned off the engine, took a deep breath, and walked to the backyard. The sun was slowly creeping westward and I took many deep, contemplative breaths. I shut my eyes and decided that I may need to be content in not knowing why. I did, however, decide in those moments that I wanted to write a book. I wanted to reach out and reach within to come to terms with the field I am passionate about, social work. This is where the book began; the idea was born in my backyard among the grass, the garden that needs my attention, the sunset, and my struggle. The book serves as a type of field guide for social workers entering the profession. The purpose of the book is to share and process the common experience of many of us in the social work field. The book is unique because it is not a traditional textbook. The book is not filled with imaginary case studies, theoretical frameworks, policy, or research but, rather, strategies to cope with and understand our clients' stories of pain and trauma in the context of real-life examples from a real-life social worker in the field.

Each chapter in the book provides anecdotal examples of a variety of social work practice experiences I have had in my fifteen-year career. It is important to note that identifying information about the clients has been changed to ensure confidentiality. As an undergraduate and, later, graduate social work student, I would have deeply appreciated the opportunity to hear about other social workers' experiences with

1

traumatized clients—what working with people in the depths of their own painful experiences was *really* like. In addition to the anecdotes I write about regarding experiences in child protection services, advocacy at a rape crisis center, and work at a Veterans Affairs (VA) Medical Center, I have listed a blend of personal and professional insights related to what I have learned about social work through my practice experiences and, primarily, what I have learned from my clients. To be specific, I share discoveries about myself in relationship to other people and how this informs my practice every single day.

The problem the book addresses is the "baptism by fire" experience most new social workers have when entering the field. More often than not, social workers sprinting out of the starting gates of their respective social work academic programs have a strongly held belief that they are now prepared to "change the world one client at a time." This certainly was my belief system as a new social worker and to some extent it may still be what I believe. I knew nothing about being a witness to the sort of pain I was about to experience with my clients. This book is a testament to the often-thankless job of social workers and other helping professionals. This book is also a teaching tool to help students studying to become social workers—both at the undergraduate and graduate levels—have a greater understanding and awareness of work with traumatized individuals. My goal is to address underlying beliefs about our clients that may lead to challenges in relationship building, increased stress for the client and the social worker, professional burnout, and compassion fatigue. This is my letter to social work students in their final year of education, especially those in internships and field placements. Agencies that employ numerous social workers might also incorporate this book for training and orientation purposes, including county social service agencies, nursing homes, hospitals and medical clinics, crisis centers, prisons, and schools. Finally, this book should be meaningful to social workers already experiencing burnout, compassion fatigue, or an existential crisis, asking themselves: "Why am I doing this work?"

In this book, I reference breakthrough moments I have had in striking a balance between my own personal agenda to "save the world one client at a time" and the reality of what occurs between me, the social worker, and my clients. I provide insights into the intense nature of the work, real-life examples that are relatable and thought provoking, and basic insights to assist social workers in embracing the role of "helper" while working to avoid compromising themselves, their professional values, and doing the work *for* the client instead of *with* them. My hope is that the reader will recognize that when we work with our clients and with their pain, we will give our clients more than we could have ever imagined and, at the same time, value ourselves and the hard work we do.

chapter one

A Witness to Pain

*"Everything has its wonders, even darkness and silence,
and I learn that whatever state I may be in, therein to be
content."*

—HELEN KELLER

M arcie and John were five sessions into marital counseling.[1]
Emotionally, they seemed to be somewhere between "Why
are we here?" and "Now that we know what we're dealing
with, what can we do about it?" I, as their therapist, had made every
effort to "move" them in some sort of direction . . . any direction.
Through challenging their beliefs about what the experience of marriage was supposed to be after fifteen years together to giving them
assignments to work on around emotional intimacy and seeking to
meet one another's needs, I had hoped to see some evidence of healing.
During many of our sessions, it was obvious that John was emotionally, psychologically, and physically leaving the relationship right before
Marcie's and my eyes. Ten minutes into each session, John's chair would
slowly and steadily start backing toward the corner of the room. Now,
it certainly could be that John, a Desert Storm veteran, suffering from
posttraumatic stress disorder (PTSD), was moving his chair out of fear,
a sense of powerlessness, or to feel safe; but in reality, as we eventually
discovered, John was leaving the relationship.

1. Names of clients have been changed in addition to some details regarding
actual client stories to protect their identities.

During session five, Marcie was adamant that once John's traumatic experiences in combat were dealt with, he would be the man she loved and had been married to for the past fifteen years. But John, as we found out in session five, was done. He was done with Marcie, with their marriage, and with the work that was being asked of him in marital therapy. Toward the end of our session that evening, I was feeling especially hopeless and frustrated about how to help this couple. In our closing minutes together, John slowly and solemnly looked up, looked to his wife, and said, "Marcie, I'm sorry. I don't love you as I once did. I wanted so badly to feel something for you again. But I don't. I can't. It's over."

John began to sob, uncontrollably, while Marcie watched in disbelief. She looked to me, a look of questioning, shock, and desperation. She numbly responded, "John. I love you. I can't believe this. I want you to be happy . . ." Her words trailed off like a car vanishing down an endless country road with only a cloud of dust remaining. The mix of anger and gut-wrenching pain was evident both in her eyes and on her face. Their pain filled the room. I watched. I listened. I silently thought, "Here it is. The end. The end of a marriage. What could I say? What *should* I say?" "*Just be with them,*" I told myself; "*Just be with them and their pain.*"

I am not sure when I began to recognize the value of being with people in their pain. As a social worker, I am a witness to pain. Being with people in pain—emotional and sometimes physical pain—is what I do. It's what I feel called to do. And so begins my journey of sharing with you, my fellow social workers, how we can witness pain, how we can be with people in their darkest moments, and in their most personal anguish, and how this experience can be life changing for both them and us. Our work is to somehow, some way, help our clients maneuver through their pain, and maybe, just as important, how we, as social workers, find our way.

The National Association of Social Workers (NASW) provides a code of ethics for professional social work practice. The code serves as an invaluable guide not only to our client-centered practice but it also provides insight into how we need to allow our clients to determine their own paths, both through their own choices and their own mistakes. To a large extent, this can be very freeing for us, the helper. The code not only guides but also validates the importance of allowing and encouraging our clients to "be in the pain." The following section of the code has helped me tremendously in my practice:

> Social Workers respect and promote the right of clients to self-determination and assist clients in their efforts to identify and clarify their goals. [NASW, 2006, §. 1.02—Self-Determination]

When we are with our clients, listening, pondering, contemplating, challenging, and helping, there are several things we can do to uphold our professional values while gaining wisdom from our clients' often-remarkable ability and will to survive. Just as we act to sustain life and survive, so do our clients. I've made numerous mistakes along my professional path, but I've also discovered some basic philosophies and insights that work. The balance between helping my clients and not sacrificing my own mental health is a fine line. It's like balancing on a high wire and we, as the helpers, decide if the net will be there to catch us or not. To care for our clients, we need to care for ourselves. (More on the issue of self-care later in the book.) And so back to my original dilemma with Marci and John—"What should I say?" Or my frequently held belief, "I need to do something, what will I do?" The following insights and experiences have occurred and evolved over time. I find them useful, simple, and straightforward.

Insight 1: Listen

Very early in my career, I was working at a nonprofit, grassroots organization that had a primary mission of advocating for victims of sexual violence. With little practical experience, but an enormous amount of compassion and drive—"I can and will change the world, one victim at a time!"—I vividly recall a hands-on learning experience with a severely traumatized woman. I responded to a crisis call in the early hours of the morning: my pager went off, my heart began to race, and I quickly learned that a victim of acquaintance rape had just arrived at the local emergency trauma center. With a belief in myself and my abilities and self-assuredness I cannot explain, I went to this woman. At just before two a.m., in the dark hours of the morning, I was quietly and quickly ushered to her exam room where I soon discovered I was very, very small. The smallness felt childlike. It's like that feeling when you walk into a room and all eyes turn to you with some sort of expectant gaze. There were only two pairs of eyes that night, one of the nurse showing me to this woman, and the woman herself. I humbly wondered to myself, "How long before they realize I don't really know what I'm doing?" I felt small in the sense that I was about to encounter someone, something . . . an experience much, much bigger than me. I was uncertain that my compassion and drive would be enough in those moments.

I began to listen. I decided that likely there were no words for what had happened to this woman. The best and most important tool I had was the ability to listen—to truly and authentically hear the words, the feelings, and the pain she was sharing with me. Me, this stranger who was there in the early hours of the morning, at one of the darkest moments of this young woman's life. I was ready to hear what she wanted to tell me. I did not and could not know her experience. I quietly and calmly introduced myself and simply said, "I am here. When you're ready to talk, I will listen."

Insight 2: Be Present

It is uncomfortable when others are in excruciating emotional pain. I grew up and continue to live in the Midwest. We have coined a phrase, it's "Minnesota Nice." What this means for me is that when people are upset, angry, distraught, or feeling anything other than fine, I tend to want to rescue, to make it okay, to make the other person comfortable. This was and continues to be a key piece of my personal and professional development. A balance must be struck between being compassionate as a helper and finding a comfort level with witnessing clients' pain.

I was in session in an outpatient mental health setting with a client who was processing very painful experiences related to childhood sexual trauma. The client began to process his self-loathing related to his experiences, truly believing he had acted in a way (at age eight) to bring the abuse on himself. "I must have said something," he recalled. "I maybe joked with him [the abuser] and let him think it would be okay [to abuse me]." As the client continued to attempt to process these beliefs and work through his painful experience, I found myself thinking about the busy day I had ahead of me. He was my first client of the day, the session had been an intense twenty-five minutes at this point and I began to drift, in my own mind, to what was awaiting me in the lobby . . . more painful stories, more clients.

The client looked at me at this point, his tearfulness interrupted my self-absorbed thoughts, and he asked, "Are you okay? Maybe I shouldn't be dumping this on you." I was dumbfounded. I was like a deer on a northern Minnesota road gazing into the headlights of an oncoming vehicle, unable to move. I realized in that moment that I was not present with my client. I was unintentionally reinforcing for him the beliefs he had held for the last forty years of his life, "I am not worth it." Needless to say, my response was open and quick. Together, we moved in the direction we needed to go therapeutically. I asked him why he was wondering if I was okay. The client responded as I feared he would, he said, "Well, it seems like you're mind is somewhere else." In fact it was. Caught. I told the client I appreciated his concern and admitted, quite honestly that I was not as present, emotionally, as I needed to be. I apologized for this and assured him that he was worth listening to and that I was going to work harder at this in the remainder of our session. I have to admit that I wanted to tell my client, "No! I'm absolutely fine. I've heard everything you've said and I am fully present with you." This response would have (1) been untruthful and (2) not given my client credit for his accurate perceptions of our work, which would have invalidated his experience.

The lesson I take from this experience is to be present, always, with our clients. It is human nature to daydream, to allow our minds to wander, to become distracted; however, it is acutely important that when working with traumatized individuals we, as helping professionals, be present with them as they share with us some of their most personal and painful experiences. We owe them our presence.

Insight 3: Be Mindful

What has never ceased to amaze me is the resiliency of the human spirit. I have heard and witnessed horrific stories of trauma, abuse, and torture in my professional work with clients and it is humbling to see and experience individuals' will and ability to survive the utmost devastating circumstances. Being mindful of what my clients have endured and may continue to endure is imperative in our work together.

An amazing young, female, Operation Iraqi Freedom veteran was in my office a few years ago, and we were discussing her recent PTSD diagnosis. She was describing nightmares, frequent panic attacks, and flashbacks related to her work as a truck driver with her unit stationed in Baghdad. She was engaged in amazingly tough work in therapy, accepting her experiences, processing and sharing her pain, and moving forward with healing her internal wounds.

During one particularly productive session, we began to discuss support systems. Who and what, specifically, in her life did she have to support her continued healing and growth? As the consummate social worker and helper, I engaged with her, brainstorming areas where she could take emotional risks, reach out to others, and continue on her very successful path. As a young veteran, she was clearly proud of this aspect of her identity and all she had accomplished in Iraq. During our brainstorming session, I openly suggested that she consider joining the "DAV Organization." She looked at me pensively and asked, "DAV? What's that?" "Well," I said, "it's a well-known organization and it stands for Disabled American Veterans. This might be a really neat group for you to join." I continued to try, not very successfully, to sell my idea. The response from this young woman will stay with me forever, a true "aha!" moment. She calmly and confidently said, "That doesn't sound like a group for me. I am not disabled."

Be mindful. Be mindful about our clients' perceptions of themselves, others, and the world. How they filter information based on these experiences is as valid as it is valuable. It cannot be overlooked and it cannot be minimized. Always be mindful of what our clients can and will teach us.

Insight 4: Do Not Judge

In my early career, I found myself in what I truly consider one of the most challenging posts of our profession. I worked in child protective services for a period of twenty-two months in an impoverished, rural, central Minnesota county and discovered the tendency of human beings to judge, to inflict our personal values, even when in a professional role, onto those individuals with whom we work.

When I was twenty-two years old, in the earliest stages of my career, my own choices and beliefs at that time found me in a brand-new relationship, unwed, and pregnant. I still consider this one of the most painful periods of my life. I became severely ill with the pregnancy, and in ruminating about my limited choices in the circumstances I found myself, tended to fuel my already wildly burning sense of self-doubt, guilt, and shame. Ultimately, I not only survived this period of my life, I thrived. I grew emotionally in ways I didn't know were possible. I was able to take something frightening and overwhelming and create something amazing. My beautiful teenage daughter has now heard this story, years and what seems like lifetimes later. She looks at me with curiosity, all the while knowing and trusting the depth of my love for her.

I was working, shortly after my son, my second child, was born, as a child protection specialist in an impoverished, rural community. One of the cases I was working on involved a young woman, Michelle, age twenty-two, who had just given birth to her third child. She was not married, she was afraid, alone, and not necessarily ready for my help. She was struggling, as I recall, with early recovery from methamphetamine addiction and had recently had her two older children returned to her custody from a foster care placement.

I walked into her building and made my way to her apartment for one of our frequent, scheduled home visits. It was just after lunchtime and I remember my mood was hopeful and optimistic for Michelle. After knocking loudly for several minutes, hearing the noise of cartoons playing on the television and children's voices inside, Michelle came to the door. My knocking had awoken her, the home was a mess as I looked around, and as I entered the apartment, my gut began to twitch. It's a sixth sense I believe we all possess. I listen to mine all the time and it's a skill I've learned to use and value in this work. Michelle immediately began to apologize for the condition of the apartment. She gave many reasons why she was waking in the early afternoon, why the children were still in their pajamas, and why I should not be concerned. I listened to Michelle and I did not realize it at the time, but I began to judge her. I began to question her abilities, her motivation, and her reasons. I began not to hear Michelle's words and became defensive with her. I was upset, even angry. I challenged her reasons and questioned her abilities. Our relationship, which had been built, tested, and strengthened over a period of nearly a year, was quickly deteriorating. What I recognize today, years later, with more experience, and certainly more wisdom, is that in many ways, I was Michelle. Her story was my story. Her struggle brought me back to my struggle . . . as an unwed, frightened parent. My pain. What I didn't recognize at the time was that I was feeling helpless that day in Michelle's apartment looking around at the mess, the chaos, and the stress. And even though I am blessed not to have had to battle addiction, Michelle's fatigue, the demands of her children, and the demands of the system, of me, were overwhelming her.

Passing judgment on our clients' experiences will damage our relationship with them. It will create and sustain a barrier to the work that could be incredibly positive and life changing. Wherever our judgments are rooted, we need to closely examine the source, where the negativity, fear, or uncertainty is coming from, and work hard to address the issues. For me, I needed to do some painful self-examination, I needed to recognize within myself my own pain, my own experiences and how my feelings seemed to closely mirror Michelle's experiences and perhaps her feelings. My judgment toward Michelle could have been disastrous for both of us, but with self-examination, accessing supervision, and always working toward heightened self-awareness, I was able to recognize within myself the work I needed to do to be effective in my working relationship with Michelle. I was going to be of no help to Michelle as long as I held on to my judgmental views.

As with all of my clients, Michelle did not need my judgment, she needed my understanding and compassion. A wise social worker once said to me, "We are only ever one step away from being a client. Never, ever forget that." Trust me, I never will.

Insight 5: Do Not Rescue

I have come to terms with the idea that rescuing my clients is one of the biggest disservices I can render. Attempts to take away that which is truly sacred, clients' personal experiences, is in the truest sense, taking away their stories. Typically, those times I've made the mistake of rescuing my clients has been when I am uncomfortable, anxious, or afraid of their experiences or of my ability to help them with those experiences.

One of the first and still one of the most valuable tools a former supervisor and great social worker gave me was, "Don't hand your clients the tissue box." This is powerful. In sessions in which my work with the client involves emotionally laden issues or we are engaged in trauma processing, for example, tears often (and hopefully) flow freely for the client. It is our tendency as helpers and quite possibly as compassionate human beings to want the painful emotion to resolve, to stop, or at least to stop hurting so much. What my wise supervisor taught me was that by handing the client the tissue box in a moment of open emotional sharing, including tears of pain or joy, is a potentially harmful disruption that could be perceived or internalized by clients as an effort to rescue them, to stop what is healing expression of feelings and very natural. Why, you might ask, does this really matter? Well, I've considered this long and hard and when it comes to rescuing, by allowing our clients their emotional expression, no matter how painful, distressing, or uncomfortable, we are in a greater sense giving them permission to have feelings, any feelings, and we are not judging them, just being with them. Ultimately, we are not rescuing, we are simply allowing. This can be a very important and powerful experience for the therapist and client in building the therapeutic relationship. The message that can be deduced from this shared experience is a message of support from the therapist, such as "I can hold your pain, and your pain is valid. But I cannot rescue you from your pain." Another validating message might be, "I believe in you. I believe in your ability to survive this pain and if I rescue you, I take this ability away from you." I have come to believe that rescuing clients is more about the helping professional's needs than about the clients' needs.

Insight 6: Be Patient

My time line for my client's healing process and expression of pain is often quite different from my client's time line. My job is to encourage, to patiently and gently nudge when appropriate, and to slow down and guide when we agree this is necessary. If we are keen listeners and observers, our clients will tell us with their words or with their actions what they need us to know about their process.

I had an opportunity one summer to assist in the development and teaching of a course for at-risk male adolescents at an alternative high school with the unfortunate reputation of being the last resort for these amazing kids. The first day of class, I walked in, looked around, and began to sense the intensity of who was in the room with me. These young men were ready, without any hesitation, to let me know they were not pleased about my presence or theirs. Survival for these kids was a priority, school, especially summer school, was way down on the list.

The group was rich with cultural and ethnic differences. African American, Latino, American Indian, and Caucasian kids—all together—all with unique stories and many of them struggling and in pain.

The group was laid out for twelve weeks, two hours per day just before lunch. According to the school and my partner, one of my social work mentors, the clear-cut goal was that each of these students would earn adequate English credit to move on to the next grade level and for many, to graduate high school.

I have kept a journal or a diary on and off ever since I was a little girl. I have always loved to write and to tell stories. I continue to enjoy writing and telling stories, and I see a real value in writing today, especially in the context of therapy and the work of healing pain. Suffice it to say, I arrived at the first day of class like a kindergartner on her first day of show-and-tell. I believed I had a possession to lift up before my audience and that I would be greeted with wonder and amazement. This was not like show-and-tell. What I had to bring, to share, was not well received the first day, or the second day, or the third week. These young men, as I discovered, were in pain. They were angry, afraid, and desperate. The battle I waged was uphill the entire way and I would not trade the experience for anything. From walking out of the room in the midst of a discussion, to loud verbal and nonverbal interruptions (sleep and even some snoring), the challenge to engage these kids was a great one. Sharing from the various writing exercises and journaling entries we asked the students to write, was always optional. On a rare occasion, several days into class, we'd get to hear amazing poetry, free writing, and autobiographical tidbits from the kids' lives.

As the hot and humid days of August came to an end, so did our class. We spent the last week of class enjoying lunches together, playing a variety of music, and the atmosphere was free—free from the worries of day-to-day life. The last day of class, I asked each student to write a brief, one-page summary about their thoughts and feelings related to the summer school class and our time together. I was taking a big risk. I believed my self-esteem was ready, even for the worst, and so I waited with baited breath for the students to finish their final writing exercise and turn it in to me before they left.

I cannot put into words what the responses meant to me. It is easier for me to share one from a seventeen-year-old American Indian student that continues to be one of the most important tools I've grasped in working with clients in pain thus far. His statement read:

Miss Sarah,

This class was good. I did not want to be here at first, because I need to work full-time to help take care of my mom and younger brother and sister. I have never had a class like this before. I never really tried journaling, but I guess it's not that bad. Maybe I'll keep doing it. Like I said in class, my people come from a long line of storytellers. Maybe I am a storyteller, too. My grandmother told me a story once about the lesson of the turtle. She said that the turtle is a wise and creative teacher. She said that the turtle buries its eggs in the sand and allows the sun, in time, to hatch them. She taught me to bury my thoughts, like the turtle's eggs. To give time and patience to my ideas before I allow them to come out.

The turtle helps me so I always remember to be patient. Anything worth having is worth my time. Thank you for sticking with our class and for not giving up on me.

Today, I have a small, stone carving of a sea turtle on my desk. I think I found it in Georgia on a trip I took a while back. The student's story, his wisdom, and his willingness to risk, are all lessons I carry with me. Having patience with our clients and allowing them to tell us and to show us what they need from us is at times challenging, but offers a richness to the relationship that cannot be forged without it.

chapter two

The Pain in the Room

"Were it not for hope, the heart would break."

—SCOTTISH PROVERB

W hen I was a brand new therapist, having just completed my graduate degree in social work, I found myself working with clients in a chemical dependency treatment program. Early on, I had the opportunity to participate as a cotherapist in one of the daily treatment groups. I was thrilled to be a part of the group and hoped I would be able to gather information about this particular therapist's style, the group's process, and how my work might be influenced.

I vividly remember an afternoon therapy group after a particular client shared his story and, quite literally, the pain was in the room. The group was quiet, some members clearly distracted, some certainly contemplative about being in treatment, some bored, and some fully engaged in the process. It was the first day of treatment and the first experience in group for one of our members. As a new group member, he was expected to share, in detail, his life story of chemical dependency, how the use had impacted his life, relationships, and how he ended up in treatment. He was clearly nervous, his legs vibrating and the papers in his hand trembling lightly; he was distressed. He looked down for much of the time. He read his story slowly, thoughtfully, as his voice quivered. I knew in those moments that I was witnessing his pain. He read from his five-page document some of the most horrific childhood abuse I've ever heard. Ritualistic abuse, beatings, heart stopping fear, and great, great sadness all poured from his pages. When he was finished, the room was silent. I looked around and all heads were low, some members had tears and some appeared to have numb reactions. The client looked up and looked to me as if to say, "What do I do now?" He said nothing. There were no words for the experiences he had shared. After what seemed like several minutes, I allowed us to use the silence to digest the story we had just heard. I looked to the client and I said, very solemnly, "Your pain has filled up this room. Your pain feels present here." He nodded, responding to my acknowledgment of what he had shared, tears continued to fall, and our group closed that day as there was little else to say.

It was extremely important in this particular example that we allowed the pain to be in the room. What that client was able to do by telling his story, his real-life nightmare, was to share his pain with others with a hope it would be lessened, certainly not minimized, but shared. The common experience of the group process allowed this to occur. The pain was acknowledged through silence. It permeated the room and we, as his group, were able to hold his pain with the hope that we could somehow lighten his load. Over the next several weeks of the treatment program, many group members entered and left the group as regularly as the clocked ticked. We engaged in the work of healing. The challenges faced by many of the group members did not begin or end in our group, but it was a safe place to stop, along their individual journeys, and ponder what it was they wanted to share, to gain, to learn, and to leave behind.

Insight 1: Acknowledge the Pain

I've been quite fortunate to have had great mentors and supervisors in my various social work positions and one tidbit of wisdom given to me about how we live with emotional pain is still used regularly in my practice today.

An effective metaphor I frequently use in therapy when working with individuals struggling with debilitating symptoms of PTSD, anxiety disorders, and chronic depression, is the "monster in the closet." The metaphor was given to me by a professional mentor, someone with a vast amount of experience treating PTSD, well beyond what I could hope to know about the disorder and how individuals cope.

Inviting the clients' trauma into session, that is, asking clients to share and process their traumatic experiences, is like asking the monster to come out of the closet. It is my belief, based on my own study of incredible therapists such as Patricia Resig, Aphrodite Mitsakis (1996), and other experts in the field of PTSD and trauma work, that if trauma and emotional pain are avoided, the pain will persist and intensify, often leaving individuals imprisoned by their painful experiences and their beliefs about how the experience influences every area of their lives. Asking the monster to come out of the closet is a skill that requires extensive clinical training, experience, and ongoing clinical consultation. For clinically trained social workers, without proper training and expertise on how to engage in trauma therapy, the monster could take over and leave our clients at risk and vulnerable. If, as a new therapist, you are interested in trauma work, it is my belief that extensive training and consultation (individual, group, or preferably both) are required.

Trauma work, when accessing the monsters, can be incredibly anxiety provoking for the client. Talking about and sharing one's most personal and painful experiences is challenging and the use of metaphor has been an effective tool when inviting the monsters into session. Teaching clients coping skills and how to live *with* the monsters versus getting rid of the monsters are key to what I believe is at the heart of trauma-processing work. Ridding oneself of the monsters is an unrealistic and unattainable goal, often leading to additional disappointment and entrenchment for the client. So how does one coexist with the monsters? Is living harmoniously the goal? An overview of this particular metaphor may be described in the following way in the initial phases of how I often engage with clients in trauma therapy:

> When you consider your traumatic experience, I want you to compare this to a monster—a big, horrible beast, with gnashing teeth, and frightening yellow eyes. Just like your traumatic experience was and still is frightening, so is the monster. It seems that the monster is overwhelming you, taking over your emotions, your thoughts, and your life. This is what has brought you to therapy. You can no longer cope with the monster and you need help.

Because thoughts and memories related to your traumatic experience are likely fear provoking, you may find yourself wanting to avoid—avoid the pain, avoid the thoughts, avoid any reminders, and avoid other people as they may not understand. Avoidance may become larger than life, isolation takes over, and your world becomes very, very small. It makes sense that you want to avoid. You may begin to believe that by not avoiding you could lose control, become overwhelmed with emotion, and lose your ability to function. Or you may believe you are unable to tolerate whatever it is you fear will occur by remembering or feeling. The challenge before us is to invite the monster (the trauma) out of the closet (out of your mind or your memory) into our sessions here, together, in order to begin the work of healing and acceptance. Through acknowledging the monster, we can begin to open the door to understanding, forgiveness of self and perhaps others, and work toward hope for the future. Once we invite the monster out of the closet, our goal will be to recognize and understand the monster's identity and its patterns of behavior. We will allow it to be present in order to learn from it and to understand how you may coexist together without fear. Figuratively speaking, our goal will be to shake hands with the monster, letting it know it can exist within you, but cannot take over your life. The monster will need to live and abide by your rules. For example, it will not be able to instill fear, shame, or any other debilitating symptom that will prevent you from living the life you want and deserve. The loud and clear message to the monster is that now and always, "I am in control." The monster can live in your closet, but under your house rules.

As a compassionate listener, I am in a position to validate and allow painful experiences to be verbalized and to assist in finding a place for the pain to linger and to rest. For the survivor of trauma to experience some form of freedom, perhaps even serenity, is the ultimate goal. Acknowledging the clients' stories and their pain is a powerful tool in setting the groundwork that is imperative in our working relationships with them.

Insight 2: Holding Pain

One of my professional passions is working with women. Women's issues, their stories, challenges, and pain have always intrigued and inspired me. I have some incredible female teachers and believe that women have an amazing internal power and ability to heal themselves, and to heal others. For several years, I have facilitated women's groups and have embraced the women's military sexual trauma group because not only have these women survived sexual trauma, but they also challenged the status quo and said "forget the traditional, male-dominated ideals of the military—there's a place for me, so move over!" The women veterans' stories of survival and achievement are impressive and inspirational.

Pain comes in many forms. Anger is one of its most powerful forms. Anger can keep us stuck or it can keep us moving. Anger, as with any emotion, is not good or bad, it just is. One particular women's group was unforgettable because the anger in the group that day was real and it was raw. Anger unleashed when it comes to issues related to revenge is like a caged tiger, seeing its prey just outside its grasp, and being trapped by the steel bars keeping its natural tendencies locked away, repressed, and controlled.

For sexual trauma survivors, revenge fantasies are relatively common and understandable. Acting on these fantasies is not adaptive and is not a healthy form of healing and can obviously have negative consequences. Discussing revenge, opening up about intense feelings of rage, anger, and a desire to get back at one's perpetrator seems natural and important in many ways. Assisting our clients in understanding anger is important and necessary in doing the work of healing pain. It is common practice for me to take the opportunity in sexual trauma survivors' groups to discuss the challenge of closure, of placing one of their darkest and most painful experiences, somewhere within their physical, emotional, and psychological self, to find peace and balance.

In group, we were focused on the issue of anger, of having and experiencing a complete loss of control during an assault, and how feeling vulnerable or out of control in other areas of life often triggers anger for many of the group members. The group's ability to share with one another, their ability to gently confront when necessary, or to quietly listen, was evident and a powerful, therapeutic tool. The group's job during this particular session was to hold the pain—the pain of the women survivors sitting in a circle, looking desperately to one another for compassion, understanding, and answers. By holding the pain, I certainly don't mean containing or controlling. Holding the pain of these women's stories and allowing its presence, including their wounds, and their most personal experiences, was of utmost value and importance. When discussing her twenty-year military career, one of our group members wondered aloud, "Why in the hell don't people understand what it's like for us? Where is our honor? We sacrificed, too." Her face was red, her voice intense and low, her teeth clenched. She was filled with rage and at any moment, it seemed, the temperature in the room could rise or fall depending on others' responses—our ability to hold her pain. There were no answers, no responses, nothing rational that could have been said during this group that would have made any sense in the lives of these women when it came to their stories of surviving sexual trauma in the military. Holding the pain was our most viable option. Our presence, our openness, and our willingness to accept her right where she was, was all we could and should do for her in those moments. The group didn't waiver. Their strength and power were incredible. Without saying it, the women let one another know "We are here and we accept your pain."

The anger radiating from the women in group was quick and it was contagious. It was imperative that I, as the facilitator, keep the group safe, both emotionally and physically, for all of the participants. In past experiences, if groups have become volatile and potentially unsafe, I have had no reservations about ending the group prematurely. Communicating to group participants that for their safety and for the health of the group, we are ending now is an important role of the facilitator. I have asked the group to reach out for support if needed prior to the next group session and then allowed time during the next session to process and debrief regarding the participant's thoughts, feelings, and reactions before working to move the group forward. Being able to end a group, redirect the group, or to interject comments and reminders about the integrity of the group, and the necessity of safety, are all required skills of an effective social worker as a group facilitator.

Being with a client in pain can potentially be an incredibly uncomfortable place for the helper. What is intrinsically important to a professionally trained helper is to assist with the problem presented, to analyze, assess, and work toward some sort of resolution. What group work has taught me, especially in this particular example, is that the resolution is often the expression of pain, including the venting, unloading, and releasing of it. Knowing all the while that there are times when there is nothing to fix or resolve, but simply being present, empathetic, and in tune, is a relief. Intensely uneasy moments preceded my realization of this important insight. Simply holding the pain for the client is sometimes resolution enough.

Insight 3: When Pain is Raw

Pain can be unexpected. It's important to be aware of our own misperceptions, biases, and judgments. Many of our clients who may have experienced one form of childhood trauma or another often have amazingly keen perceptions of others in adulthood. The ability to "read" people as safe or unsafe, trustworthy or untrustworthy, is an important skill often developed by children whose traumatic experiences, perpetrated by the adults in their lives, are the norm and not the exception.

I was working at a rape crisis center with a true grassroots mission of attempting to fill the gaping cracks in services available to victims of sexual violence and their loved ones. I had been following the care of a young woman after having been called to her junior high school by her school social worker. The school, her team of teachers, and her family, had valiantly attempted to intervene with the young woman. All felt desperate and hopeless, similar, I believe, to being in a blackened cave with no light and no direction, and a sense that there is no way out. When I went to the school for an initial visit with the young woman and her parents, I was unprepared for the high expectations the parents had for how I could "fix" their daughter. I learned a lot about parents' fearless love for their children during the experience, but I also learned that when pain is raw, it permeates everything. I was in a fortunate role as an advocate with a community agency as I did not have the power or influence of the school system, the legal system, or the family system. I was a separate and much less threatening entity and how I was perceived by the young woman made a tremendous difference in our ability to work with one another.

The young woman and I were given an opportunity to sit down together after our visit with her parents. I did most of the talking, probably motivated by my anxiety about being able to help her, how to relieve her parents, and give the school some security in knowing someone was doing something. This was an amazing young woman. She was bold, spirited, creative, and in a lot of pain. She was a cutter. She had survived sexual abuse perpetrated by an older step-sibling who was no longer living in the home. What we were able to discover over time, is that the fear and rage related to what had occurred was still very much present in the home, and within the family, especially within the young woman.

I was challenged by our ongoing, weekly meetings. I'd arrive just before her open study period and we'd meet in an unoccupied space in the guidance counseling office. Her apprehension was evidenced by her lowered head, minimal eye contact, and a pervasive sadness on her face and in her body language. I had compassion for her reservations about me as I was yet another helper whom she was certain would be unable to help with her pain. What I learned over several weeks together with the young woman, was that her family continued to question whether or not the abuse between her older stepbrother and she had actually occurred. Denial. The family was in pain, they struggled with the brokenness they both felt and experienced by the loss of their son and to a large extent, their daughter. She was still physically in the home, but was alienated and alone because of her intense feelings of self-blame, guilt, and regret. What she was able to let me know was that she blamed herself for her brother's absence from the home. She often wondered, "If I hadn't said anything and just tried to avoid him more, maybe he'd have stopped abusing me. Maybe he'd still be home and my parents wouldn't be so upset." She had told of the abuse. She had done what she had been taught, *tell and keep telling until you are believed and you are safe.*

As with many individuals who engage in self-harm or mutilation behaviors, this young woman was punishing herself. Self-injury is an all-too-common phenomenon in adolescents who have survived trauma, especially sexual trauma. The young woman's parents, because of their own intense fear and anxiety, believed the cutting behavior to be a cry for help that, in fact, was partially true; however, they also believed her cutting behavior was suicidal in nature and that ultimately, their daughter wanted to end her life. What I was able to determine over several weeks' time, was that she was not suicidal; it was incredibly painful for her to continue living as she was, but she was adamant that she did not want to die. She wanted the emotional pain to stop. Much of her cutting was on inconspicuous areas of her body, including her abdomen and upper thighs. She never, at age fourteen, had worn a two-piece swimsuit and described feelings of alienation with many of her friends who insisted she had the "body for a bikini," which further reinforced her shame and isolation. Our work focused on the processing of painful traumatic material related to the abuse, as well as a lot of time on her self-blame and guilt, truly the root cause of the cutting. When we began to discuss what behavior or action could replace the razor blades she used to harm and cut on her body, her anxiety heightened and the cutting behavior worsened. We worked through her feelings of anxiety, loss, and discomfort and with time and patience, she was slowly able to consider alternatives.

As the school year came to a close, we had forged a positive and close working relationship. I, and I believe she, enjoyed our meetings and looked forward to them. The cutting behavior had greatly reduced but was not extinguished. Her parents and the school continued to find this incredibly challenging; however, advocacy and education around the young woman's needs and continued challenges were of the utmost value when trying to heal and patch the many fragile relationships in her life. At one of our final visits, I was not prepared to experience what the young woman needed from me that day. She told me she needed to "give me something." The relationship between us, as strong as I believed it to be, was still fragile. Rejecting a gift or a token because of ethical practice guidelines might have been incredibly damaging at the time. All of these thoughts were floating around in my mind as I waited and wondered what the gift could possibly be. She dug in her sweatshirt pocket and paused for several moments before removing her closed fist and placed a small razor blade on the table in front of me. I recall a sick feeling coming over me. I was unsteady, unprepared, and unsure of what to say or do. I wasn't sure of the symbolism in those moments until much later when I had time to process what had occurred. In many ways, she was telling me about her pain, the rawness of it, the intensity with which she desperately wanted help and wanted the pain to stop. She, in an effort to tell me all of what she wanted me to know, handed me her razor blade. She had the wisdom and insight to understand that she was harming her body and even though she knew this, she was still challenged by the drive to continue. She was faced with a decision—stop what she knew worked to relieve pain temporarily—or bravely face the pain, without the tool for self-injury. She took a big step by handing over the razor blade and I'm uncertain today if she ever stopped the self-injury, but what I learned is a valuable lesson in never underestimating our clients' desire to change.

Insight 4: Client Safety

As social workers, our education, training, supervision, and hands-on field experiences serve as our guide in an often-unpredictable career. Human beings are unpredictable. Sure, there are specific diagnoses, patterns of behavior, personality traits, and so forth that lend some predictability; however, when it comes to crises, traumatic reactions, or intense levels of stress, even the most anticipated situations can quickly turn and change.

I was seeing a male client in an outpatient mental health setting for individual therapy related to the death of his son and unresolved grief and loss. The client had been hospitalized a year earlier for a suicide attempt. His pain was chronic; it had built and intensified over time. He had attempted to medicate with alcohol, with work, and with isolation; however, the pain persisted, leaving him feeling desperate and hopeless. Following his discharge from a secure, psychiatric hospital, he did well for several months and slowly began to convince himself that he was okay and that antidepressant medications weren't the answer. He could do it on his own and his stubbornness would be enough to get him through. He had been off the antidepressants for about a month when his doctor referred him to me for individual therapy. He was averse to help and again, believed his will was enough to get him through the pain. He had been through worse, he had said, this would also pass. His depression, as we learned over time, was debilitating. His physical and emotional health suffered and as the weeks passed, the therapy did not seem to be helping and his mood continued to spiral downward, his physical appearance deteriorated; his health was at risk. The thoughts of suicide had returned, he acknowledged during one of our sessions. They were passive, he told me, he didn't have a plan, but was unclear and uncertain if he wouldn't just "end it all."

Suicidal clients are difficult to work with because of the often-intense nature of their beliefs. The ambiguity with which this particular man viewed life made it especially problematic: it truly didn't matter to him, most days, if he lived or if he died. We would attempt to identify life-oriented ideas, plans, and activities, which in my office sounded great and he was all for. When he returned home, he was alone, and was welcomed by his empty house only adding to a growing despair. In session, I would ask him to "Tell me what makes life worth living today," and he would say "Well, I looked forward to our appointment. I didn't want to miss my appointment." We'd build on his response, working toward a sense of purpose, that it mattered he was there, and it mattered he was making an effort, even if the steps seemed small and ever so slow.

With time, the client was able to spend a few minutes talking about his son, his love for him, his fear surrounding his death, and the emptiness that had remained since his passing. He told me that while his son was dying, he believed he was failing him. He held onto the belief that there was something he "could have or should have" done to save him. He placed much of his judgment about being a bad father on his helplessness during his son's lengthy illness. Intellectually, he knew he could not save his son. He knew the powerlessness of the situation. Emotionally, he could not wrap his heart around this. Frequently, I have found that survivors of traumatic loss through death use self-blame to a large extent to explain and rationalize the loss of a loved one. The utter feeling of helplessness is somehow managed by the survivor and used to self-soothe, however maladaptive the soothing techniques may be viewed by the observer—the helper in this case.

We decided over several weeks in therapy that our work needed to focus on self-forgiveness and resolving, to the extent possible, the intense grief he still experienced on a regular basis. The client decided it was time to say goodbye to his son. He had a need to confess to him all he believed he had done wrong and ask for his forgiveness, with the ultimate goal of saying good-bye. We hoped this would lessen the intensity of the emotional pain he was drowning in. When engaging in the work around his grief and hearing about his pain, I was acutely aware of his previous suicidal thoughts and attempt to take his life and the importance of safety for this client. Opening up these wounds could not and would not be taken lightly by him or me. The risks inherent with trauma work are important issues that should be at the forefront of any professional's work with high risk clients.

During each session, we discussed healthy coping, what he was doing, specifically, or not doing, to take care of his emotional, physical, and psychological health. If it seemed he was not taking care of himself, then a safety action plan was developed, reviewed, and adjusted on an ongoing basis. The other key component to maintaining client safety was the opportunities I took to seek and use professional consultation and support. The client was surrounded by a team of professionals from a variety of disciplines; it was a relief to know I was not alone. I seek and utilize supervision and consultation regularly in my work. There is always a situation, a challenge, or a question that is better resolved or answered by a team of professionals versus me alone. A second key piece to helping the client open up and work toward healing his emotional wounds was my ability to be direct and honest with the client about suicide. It is an unfortunate myth that talking to suicidal clients about suicide will cause them to follow through with taking their lives. I have taken extensive training in suicide prevention and assessment and have learned that, in fact, talking about suicide has the ability to prevent the act from occurring. I often heard myself saying in session, "I am very concerned about your safety. Have you had any thoughts about hurting or killing yourself today? In the past week? Two weeks?" Through empathetic engagement, we were able to continue to build our therapeutic relationship while I was conveying my concerns that the veteran was at risk. I might say, "I am concerned you are thinking about taking your life. I hope you will talk with me about this and I hope you will share your thoughts and feelings with me." Be honest and be direct.

The pain of suicidal clients is unsettling and raw. The idea that it is more painful to live than to die is profound. The death of the client's son, his intense self-blame and guilt, and the time he needed to heal might have been overwhelming, but I did not rush him. This is an example of us, as helpers, getting out of the way of our clients' work toward healing. We can walk with them, but the key is to know when we need to be quiet, listen, and allow for time to heal—client safety always being our first priority.

chapter three

Pain's Purpose

*"What lies behind you and what lies before you cannot be
compared to what lies within you."*

—ANONYMOUS

I have had the opportunity to share in the pain with clients from all
stages of life, including young children, adolescents, adults, and the
elderly. And whether it is a child discovering everything they've ever
known—even if horrifically neglectful and abusive—is going to change
because they are about to enter a foster home, or if it's a young combat
veteran, at age twenty-one, returning from Iraq only to realize that the
world may never understand what he has just experienced, or if it is an
elderly client seeing me for depression secondary to a recent diagnosis
of Parkinson's disease—the pain is real. At times, it is invasive, it touches
you, it grabs at you, and sometimes it even keeps you up at night.

What do we, as social workers, do with our clients' pain, and their
stories of trauma, torture, heartbreak, and hopelessness? In an effort to
make sense of this for myself, I have spent my career thus far trying to
figure out pain's purpose. Why do bad things happen to good people?
Why do some people have *so* much pain? Why do we do what we do in
response to pain? What I have come up with at times gives me hope and
strength and other times renders me feeling helpless and frustrated. This
is the nature of the work. It is the work of being with people in physical, emotional, and psychological pain. I often hear myself repeating
the same thoughts to clients that I repeat to myself on a regular basis.
When, in times of crisis or stress I am feeling stuck, I work at avoiding
asking the question "Why me?" The question why is a reasonable one,

Never ask

31

but when bad things happen the "why" can keep us stuck, focused on finding answers to often-unanswerable questions. Learning to find meaning and purpose in the pain and the process of discovering now that I have had this experience, what will I do? may be the most effective response.

Not long ago, I was meeting with a Vietnam combat veteran in my office. He was describing an incredibly successful career in education that had recently ended with his retirement. His children, all successful adults of whom he was extremely proud, were still a close and meaningful facet of his life. He wondered aloud with me, "Why am I struggling now? This should be the time in my life where I look back and reflect with joy on all that's been given to me." With further probing on my part and more reflection on his part, we were able to discover that he was grieving. He had come home from Vietnam the year I was born. I openly and readily acknowledged that I could not possibly know his pain, but could and did have respect, compassion, and curiosity about his story. This is where it can begin, the process of uncovering stories, painful ones that can bring our clients closer to healing. As our session closed that day, he said something that in an often-thankless profession was an energizing force that allowed me to continue my work that day, "You're a great listener." He understood and accepted that I could not know his combat experiences, but he knew fully I was present with him, listening, supporting, and anticipating his healing.

Insight 1: Finding Meaning

It is not uncommon for family members, friends, and clients to ask me, "How do you do what you do? How do you listen to this stuff, day after day, without going crazy? Doesn't it bother you?" My responses have evolved with time. Because with time comes experience, wisdom, and more tools. There is a validating emotional experience I have when others outside the field recognize the challenge of working in the helping profession. I believe it is important work and I am proud to say "I am a social worker" even though the response may be met with "Wow, how do you do that?" or "Why would you want to do that?" I often discover a little bit more about myself and about others through these experiences. I am not always sure why I do what I do, but I believe there is meaning in it and for now, that is enough for me.

Edith Eger is an amazing woman. Several years ago I had the chance to view a homemade video recording of a talk she gave at a VA Medical Center in Nashville, Tennessee. Dr. Eger has a fascinating life story. Currently in her mid-seventies, she has accomplished incredible success against some of the most devastating odds. She is a Holocaust survivor. She is a dancer, a psychologist, and a motivational speaker. In the film I had the great opportunity to view, Dr. Eger tells the story of her life. She describes intense horror while in the depths of trauma in Nazi-controlled concentration camps in 1944. Her sister and she were the only survivors in her family, their parents had been killed. After being exiled to Europe and helped to freedom by an American G.I., she eventually emigrated to the United States, where she later met and married her husband, had three children, and pursued her doctorate of psychology.

Dr. Eger's wit and wisdom are inspiring and her insights about the resiliency of the human spirit provide a framework for how I believe we can help our clients heal. In her talk, she shared many profound insights, but one in particular still resonates with me. She said that for many years she walked around wondering how to get rid of her pain. She tried many ways, always unsuccessful, to rid herself of it; until one day she had a realization that she held the power to unlock her pain: the "key was in my pocket." She had hope, she had resilience, and she had a survivor's spirit and instinct. She simply needed to recognize this within herself. How Dr. Eger's life story and life's work affects how I engage with clients in helping them work through their painful experiences is to somehow assist them with finding meaning. Not finding meaning or purpose as a result of the painful experience or experiences tends to leave a black, empty space—space where anger, resentment, and more pain can build. I've seen it happen with clients and through my role as the listener and the helper, I want to instill a sense of hope, and sense of purpose and meaning. Ultimately, we guide our clients in this direction, they will take the lead and with time, patience, and perseverance, meaning can be achieved. My own life is evidence of this. My father is a survivor of horrific childhood abuse. He, I am blessed to say, is still one of the most important and influential people in my life. He has never once harmed me. He, I believe, found meaning in his abuse. He may not be consciously aware of the meaning he pursued, but as a father, he found purpose and ended a cycle of abuse and terror with us. He loves my brother and me; we are a part of the meaning he embraced out of a past that was incredibly dark and painful. As I see it, there are two primary choices when it comes to healing from painful past experiences. We can either (1) invest our emotional energy in trying to figure out why this thing has happened to us, all the while remaining stuck and unable to move, grow, or change, or (2) we have the option of using the pain for our life's purpose, whatever purpose that may be. If we choose to use the painful experience or trauma to help ourselves or possibly to help others, then we grow emotionally, psychologically, and spiritually beyond what we ever could have imagined and our pain serves a purpose. There is greater meaning.

Insight 2: Avoidance No More

It makes perfect sense to me that if something hurts, we want it to stop. If we know something is frightening, we stay away. If we believe we are unable to cope, we will do whatever we can to avoid the thing that is creating the discomfort. When we ask our clients to share their personal stories, their darkest moments, and their pain, we are asking a lot. Clients will find creative ways to avoid having to share their painful stories. There are many reasons not to get well, to stay in pain, and to avoid what hurts. It is our work and our challenge to assist our clients in finding value in stopping avoidance and facing whatever it is that is a barrier between sickness and wellness.

I worked for a brief period as a student and family advocate for a nonprofit agency. My primary role was to provide education, support, and advocacy to adolescents and their parents who were not experiencing success at school. Whether it was truancy, failing grades, or conflicts with teachers, the students were struggling and the parents and the school personnel were desperate to find some sort of solution. I recall working at a middle school where an especially quiet, reserved young woman was not coming to school; in fact we were lucky to see her three out of five school days. She was at risk of failing for the year and having to repeat seventh grade. Her parents had tried everything, including rewards, bribery, punishment, coercion, and ignoring—nothing worked. The behavior worsened the older she became. As I got to know her, what became evident were her incredible artistic abilities. She would scribble on the cover of her tablet, or draw on her hands, arms, and anything else she could find during our sessions. Whether it was flowers, human images, or intricate designs, her talent was noticeable to anyone who got the chance to see it. The young woman's art teacher was one of her biggest supporters and frequently offered help and assistance to the young woman to try to catch up on missed work. The teacher would frequently give positive attention to the young woman when she made it to school. The student loved art, she loved the teacher; and when I brought this information to the school counselor, we both agreed that the problems the creative young woman was having needed some sort of creative solution.

At the end of the school year, it was clear that the young woman was going to have to attend summer school. She would attend three hours each morning with the hope she could pass seventh grade. What concerned me more than her grades was the fact that she didn't belong. She had few friends and evident to the girl's parents, the school, and to me was her tendency to isolate and to avoid other students. The middle school where I met the young woman was a relatively new building and was filled with some very progressive staff making a big difference in the lives of the kids every day. I, along with the school counselor and the young woman's art teacher, decided to take a risk on behalf of the student and find out if it would be possible for her to access the art room, under supervision, during the summer school session to engage in the one thing it seemed she was really passionate about. We were pleased to discover that the school was in full support of this and were even going to provide a staff person to spend time with the young woman as often as she wanted to access the art room over the summer months. The young woman, as I understand, did show up for summer school—consistently attending every day knowing she would be rewarded with free time in the art room. She found a place to belong that summer; among the paints, brushes, and clay, she was able to connect with something that mattered to her. What enhanced her experience was that some of the adults in her life understood, they listened to what she was trying to convey, and they cared.

What occurred to me as I worked in the middle school was that as wonderfully progressive and caring as the school staff were, there was still a young, seventh-grade girl who was getting lost. She was avoiding school because of her belief that no one cared. Although I and others recognized the care and concern, the young woman was not experiencing it this way. She had been asking for help through her behavior. She was conveying her pain through action not words. Her constant avoidance of school was, as it turns out, her effort to communicate. It was up to the adults in her life to listen, without judgment or criticism, but with open minds and hearts to really hear what the young woman was asking us to do.

It is easy to blame the person in pain for their circumstances. It is the unfortunate phenomenon that if people avoid us and seemingly go unnoticed, that we can easily fall into a passive and ambivalent place. It is important that even when our clients convey a sense of hopelessness or they are lost in their pain that we do not get lost but we forge ahead, stopping perhaps our avoidance to bring forth tools for healing and belonging at every opportunity.

Insight 3: Pain as a Path

One of the most challenging things we have to do as social workers is to make peace with being powerless. Without question, we have some inferred power in our roles as helpers and in some agencies and professional roles the power is more evident than in others. What I am referring to is making peace with the fact that human beings hurt other human beings and we often have a front row seat to the pain this leaves with our clients. As social workers, we may find ourselves working independently or with teams of people all driving toward a common mission or purpose. In the variety of positions I've had, I have found the team approach to be most helpful to me and to my clients.

While I was working in the chemical dependency treatment program, I had the honor of working with an incredible psychologist and friend.

His approach to client-centered practice and his belief in the possibility of healing from pain and trauma has had tremendous influence not only in my work but also in the many lives this man has touched. I was really stuck with one particular male client at the treatment program, and not sure how I was going to be of use. The client was challenging. His behavior and attitude immediately caused alienation from other clients, he found life incredibly painful, and this poured from his mouth and his behavior. He kept others at a distance and as much as I tried to embrace this client and his pain, he was highly effective at pushing me away. It's possible he was not ready to change or that I worked harder than he did, but I know that I did the best I could. As powerless as I felt, I knew in my gut I might not be able to help him.

When I reflect on my work with this client and the many who came before and after, I am struck by the importance of the work of Viktor Frankl. Dr. Frankl's philosophical belief through his own painful life experiences and the pain he witnessed from his clients is that our pain is the path to our healing. Victor Frankl, an Austrian born Holocaust survivor, psychiatrist, and psychologist, is the founder of Logo therapy. Rather than spend time going into the specific theory and technique, because it may not be for every practitioner, I will share my experience and insights into how Dr. Frankl's (1959) work, as given to me by my colleague, has inspired me both personally and professionally. Dr. Frankl, like Dr. Edith Eger as described in Chapter Two, was a survivor of Nazi Germany and the horrors of life in concentration camps. Through his experiences, he has been able to teach countless people, including helping professionals, what he learned about finding meaning in his pain. His world-renowned book, *Man's Search for Meaning,* is an exceptional account of one human being's ability to survive unspeakable horror. From this work, we, as helpers seeking to assist our clients with their pain and trauma, can derive much insight and validation about our experiences. I strongly encourage anyone in the field to read Dr. Frankl's work. One of the most profound realizations from his traumatic experiences was his conclusion that even in the midst of the most unthinkable horror, and human suffering, life still has meaning and, therefore, suffering has meaning. This is the foundation of Logo therapy. Frankl writes about his concentration camp experience from a psychiatrist's perspective:

If a prisoner felt that he could no longer endure the realities of camp life, he found a way out of his mental life—an invaluable opportunity to dwell in the spiritual domain, the one that the SS were unable to destroy. Spiritual life strengthened the prisoner, helped him adapt, and thereby improved his chances of survival. [1959:123]

How did I use the belief in "pain as a path" with my client in the chemical dependency program who wanted to keep pushing me away and anyone else who tried to help him? After accepting where my client was emotionally, I stopped any personalization I was doing, that is, "Why doesn't he like me? I'm a good social worker. Why doesn't he want to work with *me*?" I was then able to support him in the way he needed and the power of expectation and pressure to "get better" was lessened for both of us. I needed to meet him where he was, helping him understand his emotional pain could be a catalyst for healing. One of our strategies was the identification of his strengths, all that he had accomplished and survived in his life to that point, and what he was in the midst of surviving every single day in his addiction. The client was able to recognize that he had experiences, insights, and skills that he may not have had without his pain. He embraced the idea that quite possibly he was doing the best he could with what he had and with what he knew. His addiction, as severe and as painful as it was for him, could serve as his path for healing. He had been devoting so much energy in the form of anger, rage, resentment, and self-blame, that he was often left feeling empty with no more fight left in him. He discovered in the treatment program that his path lay before him: he needed to decide if he was going to use his pain to survive or to die.

As I have discovered over time, life- and death-oriented thoughts and experiences are a regular, sometimes daily, reality for some of our clients. How will we help them in determining their paths? Perhaps being gentle with ourselves as helpers and utilizing the strengths, the stories, and the very pain that is in front of us as a path to discovery, hope, and healing is a place to start.

chapter four

Did They Teach Us About This Stuff?

"We must build a new world, a far better one—one in which the eternal dignity of man is respected."

—HARRY S. TRUMAN

I remember going to an incredible marriage therapist several years ago with my husband. I recall thinking shortly into the session that, "I want to be *her* when I finally finish my degree." She was calm, wise, and very talented. She engaged us quickly and helped us to believe we had the power to change and that power was within ourselves and our relationship.

She described her philosophical beliefs like this: we are all the creators and characters in our unique personal life stories. Our stories began in childhood, within our families of origin, and from there our roles have evolved. A multitude of factors and experiences influenced how we shaped and responded to our stories and often, as was the case with my husband and me, we were continuing to play the characters we had evolved and created over time, carrying with us the experiences from our past and re-creating our stories within our marriage and family. Narrating our own stories is an effective therapy tool and there are certain modalities created around this philosophy. How do I want my story to be told? How do I want to play out my role? How do I want my character to evolve? These are all thought-provoking questions when reviewing our lives. I wonder if I am actively participating, or perhaps sitting on the sidelines. To create change within ourselves as well as

39

within our clients, we need to recognize that with each new client and every unique interaction as helpers, we are bringing our personal stories and our clients are bringing theirs. Our stories are diverse, and our differences should be used to create understanding and, ultimately, healing for our clients. Our personal stories can also inhibit our ability to allow our clients to teach us about what they need and what they want us to know about them. Awareness about our personal stories, the character we've played and continue to evolve, is imperative in our work and our ability to be fully present with our clients.

As a bachelor's level social worker, much of my new identity was wrapped up in my ability to help others. When clients weren't receptive, were unable, or possibly incapable of accepting my help, I perceived it as something personal, something I was doing wrong. It felt like a heavy burden I was choosing to carry around and I was unsure how to let go of it. Our personal baggage can potentially weigh us down and if unaddressed will get in the way of our goal of client-centered work. Personalization is a slippery slope in our work; we are forging and creating relationships with our clients all the time. Establishing rapport, trust, and understanding is key to getting the work of healing accomplished. Awareness of our own limitations and perhaps our unrealistic expectations is a difficult but imperative ongoing professional process. I suggest that we as helping professionals review our stories, reflect on who we are as the characters and creators of these stories, and always maintain self-awareness about how this affects our work.

Insight 1: Gathering Knowledge

Child protection social work was more than likely one of the best professional learning experiences I've had in my career thus far. I did not understand the cycle of human tragedy, the enormity of the system, and the clash between the two until I was immersed in the work of child and family services and the foster care system. There was nothing in my life or my education that could have prepared me for the feeling of taking the hand of a small child, literally, and walking out of a courtroom while the child's parents screamed in anguish that we were "stealing their child." No textbook, classroom lecture, or volunteer experience had prepared me for the emotional growth and painful challenges I would experience. It is not uncommon in the social work field and especially in child protective services to be asked by our clients, "Do you have kids?" I was caught off guard and a little defensive the first time I was asked this question. It is an easy question to take personally and a hard question to answer. Stylistically, as with most approaches, we will vary as professionals in how we respond. We might ask the client, "I'm not sure why this is important in our work together, can you tell me why this is something you want to know?" Or, we might simply answer the question and move forward. I have done both. The question is one we can trip over if we allow ourselves to, and you can be certain I've stumbled plenty of times. It is my belief that the question needs to be considered within the context of the relationship.

As a child protection social worker, I was frequently in a position of perceived and very real power. As much as I worked on trying to create a balanced, cohesive, give-and-take relationship, I was still a representative of the system, and I had the ability to make decisions and recommendations that affected people's lives. Trying to deny this (as I often did) will only result in additional stress and a lack of authenticity in the working relationship. Acknowledging the power imbalance, recognizing it, and stating it with my clients was freeing in many ways. I remember telling one of the parents I was working with, "The system is now in your life due to some challenges within your family. I am acknowledging that you want the system out of your life, including my role in your family's care. Let's work together to make that happen." The approach defused tenuous situations, created understanding, and established a very clear, concise goal. Being compassionate combined with a direct approach will create relief for the family and validate their discomfort with social service involvement. Another incredibly stress-reducing act on the part of the social worker is admitting what we do not know or understand. Early on, I placed tremendous pressure on myself to have all the answers. The reality is, we do not and cannot know what is right or best in every situation. The bottom line with child protective services is the safety and well-being of children and this must drive every single decision. Many social work students I've encountered over the years have aspired to work in child protection. This is an admirable goal and one that cannot be taken lightly. My time in county social work was short, only twenty-two months, and I believe today this is likely because of my inability to reconcile my social work values with the expectations and demands of the role. I give tremendous credit to those who engage in this work. It is an honorable profession.

Another example comes to mind when I consider how I have stepped outside my comfort zone in a quest to gather more professional knowledge. Often what occurs is that my quests not only lead to increased professional knowledge, but to amazing life-changing personal experiences. As I searched for a clinical field placement (internship) after completing my Master of Social Work (MSW) coursework, I comfortably looked at agencies and organizations that served children and families. Up to that point, it is what I knew and was certainly within my professional comfort zone. I'm not sure when it occurred to me (undoubtedly I have a professor to thank) to look outside the familiar to truly push myself personally and professionally. My placement search landed me in a most interesting place—a VA Medical Center.

I vividly recall driving onto the grounds of the VA Medical Center the morning of my placement interview. The driveway is almost a mile long, lined on either side with beautiful varieties of towering pine trees that have been there much longer than I have been alive. I was intimidated and anxious, my heart pounded with every movement closer to this larger-than-life, daunting place. My fears, as I have since realized, were stemming from the unknown: the uncomfortable and foreign experience of any new environment and engaging with people who are unfamiliar. It is a difficult but invigorating experience. After all, I was a young, female therapist, a nonveteran, a nonaddict, and clueless. But was I *really* clueless? It would be left to time and moving in the direction of my fear, rather than away from it, that would lead me to this growth and discovery. From the day I entered the VA Medical Center through the present day, I have continued to learn many important skills and strategies that serve me well, especially humility: admitting what I do not know, acknowledging what I do not understand, and avoiding any sort of pretending that leads to false pretenses and limited opportunities to grow. There is a tremendous relief in admitting what we do not know or understand. It has taken me a long time to embrace this concept.

Early in my career, I placed an immense amount of pressure on myself as the "professional." As stated earlier, it's okay not to have all of the answers. It's okay to be a student, a learner, and a new social worker. I'm still new, still learning, and still evolving. It's a process and there is much relief to be found in this mind-set. My first weeks at the VA Medical Center were filled with wonder and curiosity. The military was an unknown entity to me, and I wanted to soak up like a sponge all I could. The wisdom, life experiences, and insights of our clients will guide us in our work. With a little bit of humility, we will have endless learning opportunities if we can let go of our own fear and insecurity. I believe experience is the best teacher. Gathering knowledge often requires doing something different and pushing ourselves beyond the comfortable limits we place on ourselves. One of my favorite quotes by Maryanne Radmacher is hanging on a wall in my home, it reads "Change of any sort, requires courage" (2008).

Insight 2: Being Human

On many occasions I have wondered where the line is between being the professional and being human. By being human, I mean being real with clients, being approachable, and being authentic. I believe fully that we need to encompass all of these traits with our clients. The individuals with whom we work need to be able to trust us, our professionalism, our recommendations, our thoughts, and the decisions that affect their lives. Our clients need to know our role in their lives and to have clarity about how the relationship works. We, as social workers, need to take the lead in this process. Often, what makes the line between being the professional and being human blurry, is the intimate and frequently intense nature of the work we do together. We are asking our clients to share some of the most personal details of their lives to examine, process, and determine how things need to change. Consider for a moment what we are asking our clients to do. We are asking them to tell everything to someone (us) whom they know nothing about other than the basics, such as name, agency, title, and job duties. The dilemma we face is how we can be human and maintain the necessary professional boundaries in a healthy, productive, working relationship. It starts with knowing ourselves well. Recognizing our motivation, understanding our purpose, being clear about our beliefs and our professional roles, is acutely important to be prepared when precarious situations with out clients arise (and they do). Some of the challenging and uncomfortable moments I've experienced are when I have been in my clients' homes. The environment is theirs, and I am a guest. Certain professional roles have created tension for the client and for the relationship and so being the guest is not always a mutually pleasant experience. Finding creative solutions to resolve tension is a learned skill, and it is culturally acceptable to come together with food. Food, as we know, is a binder, a common experience that is celebrated and embraced in most areas of life and in most cultures. Going into clients' homes as a child protection social worker, for example, is no exception. Even in the most trying or emotionally charged situations, when the home visit was planned, it was common for the client to offer, at a minimum, coffee, and usually some sort of food. My child protection experience was in a rural area and the offering of food and drink was the norm, not the exception. As we know, our work is dependent on relationships. Our relationships, no matter how challenging, are heavily influenced by our clients' perceptions of us, including our humanness and our approachability. I cannot tell new social workers who encounter these types of circumstances what to do or what the right decision might be. It's important to consider the client, the environment, and the context. Primarily, the clients' needs and our professional role in their lives need to drive the decisions we make, even when it comes to coffee and cookies. Is having the coffee my client offers me going to strengthen our therapeutic relationship? Is having the cookie going to place my client at risk or compromise our working relationship and professional boundaries? With my clients' needs and our purpose in mind, I have had many, many cups of coffee and on occasion some really tasty cookies. Relationships are built with our clients through our thoughtfulness and respect for them, their experiences, and their stories. Regardless of our role in their lives, we can engage on a human level while remaining the professional our clients need and expect us to be.

Insight 3: You Can't Teach Compassion

There are people in every profession who misrepresent or mistreat the profession and there are social workers I've encountered who give social work a bad name. A close friend of mine is a supervisor in a human services agency and she is frequently challenged by her child and family social workers. She shared with me, while chatting over lunch one day, that she had recently held a staff meeting and asked her social work staff, "Where's your passion? Why are you choosing to work here? Why does this matter to you?" I told my friend a story about a supervisor I once had who told me that although we may not always know what to do or have the answers for our clients, what matters is that we have the heart for the work.

As I reflect on my former supervisor's wisdom and consider if I have the "heart for the work," it seems natural to turn to the ethical principals outlined in the code of ethics (NASW, 2006, pp. 5–6). The ethical principals are based on the core values that make our profession what it is. It's incredibly important to highlight the values of the profession as we consider our life's work, asking ourselves if these are values we can embrace and live out fully in our work with people. The values section helps me do some professional self-examination, which is something I find useful and necessary on an ongoing basis. The values are outlined as follows, including questions I encourage you to consider as you reflect on your own practice.

Value: Service

As a social worker, am I selflessly offering my skills and abilities to the people I serve? Do I set my self-interests aside to benefit others? Do I seek opportunities to help others with no expectation of receiving anything in return?

A good friend and co-worker is a wonderful example of someone who lives out the values of the profession. My social worker friend and colleague has been in the field for nearly forty years and is involved in numerous community organizations that reach out, on multiple levels, to various populations in need. Whether it is collecting cans of food or cash for a food drive or taking clothing donations for individuals struggling with homelessness, my friend can be found at the center of what is perpetuating service to others. What is especially notable about his work is the tireless but unwavering assistance he offers with no expectations of what will be returned, often he expects nothing because he knows and believes in the value of service to others.

On occasion, I am asked to speak at local human service-type events and recently was asked to talk about anger management issues at our local National Alliance on Mental Illness (NAMI) chapter meeting. It is opportunities like these that are important to grasp. It is where we can broaden and engage in our mission of service to others as social workers, taking time to speak to what matters and doing something of value, no matter how small or insignificant it may appear. Service in social work means being responsive to the needs of others, the community, and the profession, even when we're not punching a time clock.

Value: Social Justice

In my practice, do I maintain awareness of oppression and how power and control influence my clients' lives on all social levels? Do I take advantage of opportunities to advocate for my clients when I see systemic barriers preventing them from attaining the positive health and well-being they seek? As social workers, macrolevel involvement, including belonging to professional organizations that promote our work in the field such as NASW is an excellent opportunity to maintain awareness about social issues pertinent to our work and our role as citizens. For example, involvement in our local and national political system is an area where professional networking can provide the outlet to have our voices heard and our opinions shared. Involvement may include e-mail and letter-writing campaigns, networking with other professionals about social action opportunities at the local, national, and global levels. Awareness of social justice issues that affect our clients but also our profession and how we are represented and perceived are key aspects to social work professional values.

Value: Dignity and Worth of the Person

Am I not only accepting and acknowledging my clients' right to self-determine but also, further, supporting and promoting it? As long as clients are acting socially responsible and aren't putting themselves or someone else in harm's way, am I working to assist in the development of the clients' independence from various systems? As social workers, we have a dual role (not to be confused with dual relationships). We have a responsibility to assist our clients with the changes they want to make and we have a responsibility to influence and work to eradicate the barriers that exist for our clients, which may be preventing them from achieving their goals. The well-being of our clients is influenced at all levels, including micro (individual relationships), mezzo (community), and macro (systems). For example, I have worked with female clients, both adults and adolescents, with eating disorders. I am not an expert in this area, but carry awareness about the numerous social factors that influence this painful experience for those who suffer with it.

Recently, this awareness was reinforced when I had the opportunity to participate in a workshop held at a church in my local community. I was engaged on multiple levels: as a mother of an adolescent daughter, as a concerned woman about how women are treated and perceived within our society, and as an impassioned social worker interested in the implications for my professional role. The workshop encompassed all the best of what grassroots community organizing can be. A social issue has the power to invite and challenge us while working toward cultivating change. In the case of the church's workshop, body image and self-esteem issues for women, girls, and those who care for them were being highlighted and addressed. The workshop, created by an inspirational woman within the church community, was an opportunity for me to participate, to benefit personally, and to give back professionally. The mission of the workshop was fully in line with my values as a mother, community member, and social worker. It is an exciting experience for me when these opportunities arise and become integrated. We, as a collective group of concerned citizens, were able to provide an environment of learning, growth, and possibility for a multitude of girls and women who aspired to believe in their own worth and dignity and to honestly look at these issues in a safe and supportive place. Opportunities to be a part of something where I can use both my professional and nonprofessional roles to benefit others are important to me and to my ongoing development and growth.

Value: Importance of Human Relationships

The key to our work from where I stand is the relationships we have with our clients. We can and do have a positive influence on the clients' desire to make their circumstances better with the foundation of our relationship with them. It is a basic human need to want to belong in the world—to have our place and understanding of that place, to know and realize it matters that we are here. Through small, relatively effortless ways, we can help our clients experience a sense of belonging. For example, it is very important to me to greet others in the morning when I get to work. Whether it's a co-worker, delivery person, or client, it matters to me that I notice them, acknowledge their presence, and offer a "good morning," "hello," or simply a smile. For our clients, being recognized and respected is significant and important in our ability to form relationships with them. It is easy to get wrapped up in our work, the busyness of our days, and the demands placed on us as social workers. The essence of forming a human connection—a relationship—will get lost if we don't make an effort to hold on to it. I notice when others take an interest in me: it matters that I went to work that day, that I have a place, and that I belong.

I recall entering work on a particularly snowy Minnesota winter day, the temperature outside was frigid and I had just come into my office after an icy and treacherous commute. Work was not on my mind, I was not fully present or ready to start the day. What helped me on that particular day and what continues to help me become engaged in my work and to feel prepared for the day is to make simple and pleasant connections as my workday begins. I remember a familiar client to our clinic was in the lobby and had just come in as well, waiting patiently as the clinic staff arrived that morning. He greeted each and every employee who walked through the door. As I headed toward my office, I could hear him: "Good morning, Mary," "Good Morning, Dave—looks like you had a tough drive in, glad you made it in safely," "Hi Sarah, how are you today? Boy, you sure look cold, why do we live here again?" As the client persistently and happily greeted the employees, I could see the frustration and tension melt, literally, with each of his statements.

Relationships are key to our work, and it often begins with a small connection with our clients and leads us through the important work we will do together.

Value: Integrity

Social work is about ethics. Behaving, communicating, and representing ourselves as professional social workers is a privilege. Being authentic and honest in our communication with our clients, such as not suggesting we have all of the answers all of the time, is an act of integrity: "I don't know the answer to that, but I will work to find out *and* I will get back to you." It means doing what we say we will do or walking the talk as many of my mentors have shown me through their work and their examples. As a representative of the profession, it is our duty to behave in a way that strengthens our social work identity. Whether it is participating in a staff meeting at my agency, attending professional trainings and conferences, or during nonwork hours how I am presenting myself and representing my profession, should be at the forefront of who I am. I received an e-mail the other day at work from our data-privacy expert. It was addressed to all employees and the message identified that professionals, when outside the work setting and during off-duty times, had been talking about patient-related information and that this was not only unacceptable but it was also unethical and potentially illegal. I try to remember the golden rule, would I want to be treated the way I am treating my clients? Whether my clients are in front of me or not is irrelevant when I consider the value of my professional integrity.

Value: Competence

It is imperative that we are always increasing our knowledge about our social work roles. Our field is dynamic, constantly changing and evolving. What we knew as effective and best practice ten years ago may be different today. Am I up to speed on the latest research? Am I taking the time to review the latest literature about the approaches I use with my clients? Are my clients getting the best treatment I can give them?

Cultural competence is a great example of how, historically, we would participate in a one-time cultural diversity training and somehow consider ourselves competent to work with culturally diverse clients. The two most important pieces of culturally competent practice are self-awareness and other awareness. To work toward becoming a culturally competent professional, we need to engage in ongoing education and not a one-time training or in-service. The process of self- and other awareness evolves just as we as individual social workers change; so do our clients, and it is our responsibility to pursue cultural competence on an ongoing basis.

The reality is that our profession, our country, and our world is constantly changing and we need to stay attuned to how change affects our clients and our work together. A few ways in which I work on maintaining professional competence include:

- Professional licensure—some agencies do not require social workers to maintain their professional license, which is unfortunate. Our license creates and enforces a standard of care that brings our profession to a level of competence and professionalism that is not only good for us but also good for our clients.
- Continuing education—as licensed professionals, our social work state boards require continuing education credits for us to maintain our license to practice. Finding educational opportunities that will challenge us, enhance our knowledge base, and create in us the ability to be better and stronger in our field needs to be the driving force behind what motivates our pursuit of continuing education.
- Professional consultation—this is not only important for the licensure process but also invaluable for ongoing professional growth and development. We cannot engage in the practice of social work as a lone practitioner and expect to be effective or survive the challenges the field brings to us. Consultation is imperative to our work and we all need places to access support and guidance.
- Understand and abide by the code of ethics—recently, the Minnesota Board of Social Work, with whom I am licensed, has mandated two hours of ethics training each two-year licensing cycle

for all licensed social workers (at all licensure levels) in our state. This is an exceptional change and I do hope other states follow suit. There are frequent predicaments in our work and it is inevitable we will experience challenges and precariousness because of the fact that we work with complex human beings and situations. The code of ethics is our guide and should be understood and consulted frequently to maneuver through our field in the most effective and ethical way we can.

• Educate non–social work co-workers, managers, and supervisors about the social work profession and our capabilities—we have opportunities at every turn with the general public and those individuals within our given agencies to educate about the field of social work. Misperceptions and stereotypes exist about what social workers do and don't do; explaining our roles and the unique and rewarding work we do is a great way to maintain our competence as social work professionals and enhance the general understanding of our valuable roles.

chapter five

How Do You Do What You Do?

*"Do all the good you can, by all the means you can, in all
the ways you can, in all the places you can, at all the times
you can, to all the people you can, as long as you ever can."*

—UNKNOWN

M y mother often tells me that I started my social work career at
age nine. She lovingly tells stories of how I was always compassionate as a child and desired to help others. She will say,
"That Sarah, she has always been a great listener." Whether it was my
grandparents, neighbors, or friends in some sort of personal crisis, my
drive to help has always been an internal force. Many family members
and friends, when I proudly announced I decided to become a social
worker, voiced genuine concern with my chosen career path. There
were numerous comments about the pay: "You won't make any money.
How will you survive? Do you *really* want to do that?" I, still convinced
that it wasn't about the money, would smile, agree that yes, perhaps I
wouldn't find financial wealth in my work, but was fully prepared to
find other types of wealth, far beyond what my concerned and doubtful
loved ones believed.

The money concern is valid. If you choose social work, even in
administrative or clinical positions, the pay is not at a level where you
will know enormous wealth and affluence. I think the thing that draws
certain people to the profession is also what leads people to meaningful life's work without concern for making a large salary. Don't get me
wrong, however. I do want to make a comfortable living and early in
my career I wasn't sure this would happen. I worked for a grassroots,

53

nonprofit organization that survived on private donations, fund-raising, and the occasional grant. Luxuries like raises were never really considered; we were in it for the passion of helping others. This worked beautifully until I had children, a mortgage, and day care costs. We all hope and strive to make a decent living and make a difference in the world and so far, I've been able to make it work. Continuing my education has helped financially and I believe this is true in most professions. As it turns out, my family and close friends, to some extent, had legitimate concerns about my livelihood, but they have also had the opportunity over the years to see me grow as a person and I think they all agree that social work has been the right choice for me.

Insight 1: Validation

I was blessed by the opportunity to attend a thought-provoking professional conference a few years ago with a focus of working with returning combat veterans from combat zones in Iraq and Afghanistan. The theme of the conference was the importance of the work we were doing and the challenges of encountering acutely traumatized individuals returning from war. Several speakers posed these questions in a variety of ways: How will you be effective in your work? What do you need to do personally and professionally to be the dedicated individual our returning troops need you to be? The third and final day of the conference was dedicated to "self-care strategies for the helping professional," a topic I struggle with frequently and that at the time was especially important in my work. I was really looking forward to day three, not only because I was anxious to return home to my family when the training was over and to get back to work to implement some of the things I had learned, but also because self-care has not always been something I've been very good at. The morning began as the others had, a great continental breakfast, an endless supply of fresh coffee, and now some familiarity with the fellow helping professionals seated at my table. The six people around our table were an eclectic mix of ages, ethnicities, and backgrounds. It was poignant as I looked into their faces and got to know those next to me because their faces and their stories represented our work, the immersion every day of being with others who appear so different, but in fact have common threads woven throughout our experiences. There was a sense at my table over the three days that we were all in this work together, which is another great reason to attend trainings and conferences. It is an opportunity to network and to be with people to a greater or lesser extent who "get it" when it comes to the challenges we face in the field.

The speaker for day three's topic was bright and upbeat and did an excellent job of checking in with the audience. Her formal talk began with a statement I did not see coming and will certainly never forget. She said, "People in the helping profession are often codependent personalities." *WHAT?* I thought to myself as I looked at my peers around the table. *Is she talking to us?* I had not once considered myself codependent either on a personal or professional level. This was news to me as I quickly put up some defenses. Fortunately, I was shaken enough to be intrigued by what she had to say and was able to gain some incredible self-awareness and insight into why, on numerous occasions, I have come home from exhausting days at work asking myself, "How am I going to go back tomorrow?" or "Why am I doing this work?"

As a social worker, I place a tremendous amount of importance on my professional role in the client's success. Whatever the issue, crisis, or concern may be, I frequently find myself bordering dangerously close to working harder than my clients. This is more true in certain professional settings than others; however, it is easy to fall into the trap because the core of what we do is helping. To be useful and effective, we need to know when we are helping and perhaps when we cross over into enabling or doing *for* the client instead of *with* the client. This is the issue the speaker was addressing and the most important piece was the implication this has for issues such as professional burnout and compassion fatigue. Our success and sense of satisfaction in our work cannot be entirely dependent on what our clients choose to do or not do to resolve their painful circumstances. We can celebrate with our clients when they experience successes. We should recognize the hard work we do and take credit, when appropriate, for meeting our clients halfway, being the guide, mentor, teacher, advocate, or counselor they need us to be. It is when we begin to lose sight of our role in our clients' lives that we may find ourselves on a codependent slippery slope. Our success in our work is not dependent on our clients' success. We may be highly effective in our work, and our clients, for a multitude of reasons, may not achieve the success we had hoped for or expected. Our clients define this for themselves. If we as social workers can objectively view ourselves and our work and honestly say, "I did the best I could for my client with what I had and what I know," then we can be satisfied with the outcome without it being dependent on the numerous factors outside our control. It is when we make this separation for ourselves that we can truly be free to love the work and be inspired by it.

Every once in a while you might hear or you might even hear yourself utter the words, "social work is a thankless job." This is only partially true. If we look for thank-yous or seek constant validation, we will only discover emptiness and discontent. If we embrace the moments where we know, deep inside ourselves, that we made a difference, we will carry this with us for a very long time. The "making a difference" part is what sustains me. I have, on occasion, received notes or cards from clients sometimes years after I had been a part of their lives. A former supervisor told me about a tool he had developed for himself after learning it from his supervisor early in his career. He called it his feel good file. The feel good file is an ingenious thing and since creating my own file, I have found myself wandering back to it over time, looking through the bits and pieces of my young career, finding an immense amount of joy, pride, and validation tucked away in my office drawer. Inside the dirty and worn manila file folder I have collected over fifteen years' worth of notes, cards, awards, certificates, pins, and pictures that remind me why I do this work. It only takes a moment after looking in my feel good file to experience my spirits lift and my mind wander back to moments with people who have made me a better person because of the richness this work has brought me. I encourage everyone in the helping field to create their own file to remember why it matters that we do what we do.

Insight 2: Why Me?

During an agency staff meeting at a job I held several years ago in a nonprofit agency, my social work supervisor engaged our team of social workers, psychologists, and support staff in a team-building exercise for the dual purpose of reaffirming why we were choosing to work with children and families in crisis and to allow for a break in the day-to-day challenges we faced in the field. Our supervisor asked us to count off and arrange ourselves in smaller subgroups, with the task of answering the assigned question he had prepared for us prior to the meeting. Our group was made up of three men and two women; an interesting mix because most professionals in the agency were women, which, as we know, is typically the norm for our profession. Men bring a unique and necessary perspective to our work and I have had the honor of working with many highly effective and admirable male counterparts in my career.

As our small-group discussion began around our chosen questions— "Why do you choose to do this work?" "If you could change professions, what would you do and why?"—there was an interesting variety of responses from our group. The discussion was rich and brought up several issues involving professional self-examination and self-awareness for me. When it got to my turn to respond, I said, "I don't know why I do this work." Some of my group members acted a bit surprised and others nodded with a knowing "I can relate" kind of look. I couldn't find the words in those moments to answer the question "why?" or as I was interpreting it at the time, "why me?" I recall the work I was doing as especially challenging and emotionally charged. Families in crisis, as we know, can mean numerous things; what I tended to find were families literally in some of their darkest moments. Whether it was recent acknowledgement of abusive relationships within the family or financial crises including lost jobs, homes, and security, my work was intense and the families in pain. What I failed to acknowledge at the time was the value of my role in my clients' lives. I, as I often have, placed my sense of success on the family's success. I, however, was the one defining what success meant and my expectations were far greater and unrealistic than they should have been.

As our small group continued to process and struggle with the question "Why am I doing this work?" I remember a group member and co-worker state something that made a lot of sense to me and express what I believed at the time but couldn't put into words. He said that he wasn't sure why he did the work, but he knew that he felt called to do it. He countered the original question with, "Why *not* me?" which I thought was incredibly powerful. He went on to say that he always knew he wanted to help people. He knew he was effective when it came to problem solving and had this innate ability to remain calm in the midst of others' crises. He believed he could be of use and this, at that point in his career, was enough for him. He's right, why *not* me? I have determination and drive to help others. I have compassion for the oppressed, and I am moved to action by this. I believe people can change and improve their lives and have a desire to do so. I believe if given the opportunity, people will overcome even the most devastating circumstances. I know this because I've had the good fortune of being a part of it. If we can find a way as social workers to accept the gift of our profession, we will be better able to embrace and survive the work. By the gift, I mean those times when we get to witness our clients' healing right before our eyes, where there is a recognition that "I can get through this," or the shift we see over time and through our relationships with our clients in which they become the leader and we become the follower, or the cheerleader as I like to refer to my role in those moments. Or the rare gift we receive when we hear from our clients years later and they are doing well and want us to know. I've received this particular gift and it never leaves me.

It was about five years ago when I was home on a quiet evening reading a book after having just tucked my kids into bed. The phone rang and I leisurely went to answer wondering who might be calling at this time of night. I didn't immediately recognize the voice on the other end of the line. It was a female voice, soft and pleasant yet pensive, "Hello? Do you remember me?" I didn't have a clue who it could be and said that I didn't recognize her voice. She said, "It's Katie . . . I hope its okay that I called you at your house. I really wasn't sure I should, but I found your number in the phone book because I've been thinking about you lately and I guess I just thought I'd try and it's really you!" She continued to talk quickly and nervously, sounding unsure she should have made the call. Katie, as it turned out, was a former client of mine. I worked with her while working in a job with at-risk youth at a junior high school. Katie was an incredible girl. She had a challenging life at home, and school was never really a priority for her. She had begun to experiment with marijuana and sex during the eighth grade, and when she was referred to me, I was challenged and amazed by the wisdom she exuded that was older than her years and her sometimes overly confident belief that she could do anything she wanted. She was fearless.

The night of Katie's call she told me she was compelled to call and tell me how she's been since we had met several years earlier because in her words she was "doing pretty damn good." When she began to hear in my voice that I was pleased she had called, she immediately sounded calmer, more at ease and ready to share her story. She said that the rest of her junior high and high school career as really rough; she had dropped out of school her junior year because of failing grades and the fact that her marijuana experimentation had escalated into daily abuse and included alcohol abuse as well. She had found part-time work after leaving school and to her dismay had become pregnant at age seventeen. At this point in our telephone conversation I began to wonder where her story would lead and if she was still chemical dependent. I worked to keep my mind open to the possibility that Katie's story would end differently than it had begun and so I continued to wait and patiently wonder how her survivor's instincts served her in her struggles.

Katie went on to tell me that she had had the baby and left the relationship with the child's father because of some emotional abuse. Katie shared details of the twists and turns her life took until she finally found an opportunity to enter chemical-dependency treatment. Her child, she proudly told me, was a spitting image of herself and had the same fearlessness I so clearly remembered about Katie. After treatment she was able to study and receive her General Equivalency Diploma (GED) and was enrolled in college. Katie said, as I clearly was hearing, it had not been an easy road for her. She was in a new relationship, a healthy one, and continued to battle clinical depression but was clean and sober and giving her best effort to make her life better. What came next was a touching surprise that I had not remembered as I was talking with Katie and that was her reminder to me that I was pregnant at the time of our work together. As an eighth grader, Katie had told me she would "never have children." Now, years later, Katie excitedly told me that is exactly what led her to call me and tell me what a great mom she was and how she looked to me as a role model. She did not specifically recall my role in her life at the time, "How did I meet you anyway?" she asked that night. Amazingly, the work we did on improving her grades or school attendance was not what Katie remembered all those years later, it was the modeling I did for her and the relationship we had that affected this young woman the most. As quickly and unexpectedly as Katie had called me that night, she needed to go and tend to her daughter and her schoolwork and so we said our goodbyes and I wished her well-deserved success and happiness.

Sometimes, in the midst of our work together, we don't know what our clients need to learn from us. But if we're lucky enough to hear from them, even years later, we get to have a glimpse into what role we played in their lives and sometimes, like my late night phone call, we get to learn that what we thought we knew turns out to be something else entirely. Initially, I thought I should tell Katie she couldn't call me at home, but my gut instinct told me she was sincere and knew her boundaries could not allow her to continue to call. It was wonderful to hear from her and although I have not heard from Katie again, I know that for a moment in the life of an eighth-grade girl, I gave the gift of unconditional caring and compassion and it was returned many times over by her voice on the other end of my phone years later.

Insight 3: Hope (Pandora's Box)

The inspiring part of our work is that we not only witness pain but we also witness hope and healing. I remember hearing the Greek mythological story of Pandora's box when I was in high school. Our English teacher spent a few weeks during the school year reviewing tragic Greek characters and how mythology can teach us about the complexities of behavior, instinct, and survival. My teacher was incredibly expressive; she wore her emotions on her face and in her body language. Her arms flowed upward in excitement as she proclaimed story after story of Greek heroes and heroines. I struggled as a teenager to find my place in the world. As a highly sensitive and deeply philosophical child, I was frequently raw with emotion and those in my life tended to hold on for dear life when my emotions emulated a twisting and turning rollercoaster ride. It was a timely lesson in my life; I was ready to hear the story of Pandora's Box then, and I have told the story of Pandora—of her pain, her dilemma, and her choices—many times to my clients. For our clients, hope may seem impossible or unattainable in the midst of pain and suffering. It is a gift to be able to have a job that works to inspire hope and healing in others. If you are not familiar with the mythological tale of Pandora's box, allow me to retell my version as I might in a group session with traumatized clients:

Pandora was a breathtakingly beautiful woman in Greek mythology. Her beauty was known throughout the land and she was wanted and desired by many. Pandora, as is known, was created by the great god Zeus after he became enraged with his sons, Prometheus and Epimetheus, for bringing destruction, fire, and pain to humankind. Because humankind was suffering terribly as the result of the dissention between Zeus and the brothers, Zeus ordered Pandora to be created to somehow bring peace to the brothers, to stop the pain between them, and to bring some relief to the world. Zeus ultimately gave Pandora to Epimetheus as a gift, at the same time placing the pain, destruction, disease, and death from humankind in a box for Pandora for safekeeping. Pandora was told never, under any circumstances, to open the box because of the pain that was held inside and if unleashed would only cause utter devastation to all. As the story goes, Epimetheus left Pandora alone one day with the box, which led to her intense curiosity and longing to find out what was inside this very important box. While Epimetheus was out, Pandora could not contain herself and slowly opened the box. What occurred Pandora could not understand; she immediately realized what she had done was very, very bad, but she was unable to close the box. It was too late. What was unleashed from the box was unimaginable pain and suffering. The darkness, toxicity, and utter pain that was rushing rapidly and steadily from the box into the world was like nothing Pandora had ever seen. The darkness encompassed abuse, addiction, loss, shame, abandonment, sickness, rage, and the worst imaginable human suffering.

Pandora was devastated about what she had done. She wept and cried out, "How could I have done this to the world? Now what will I do? How will we survive all of this pain that has been unleashed on us?" As Pandora sat helplessly, not knowing what she would do next, the darkness slowly began to subside. She noticed that as the toxicity was releasing itself there was a small, white, luminescent light coming from the bottom of the box. The lighted figure was small and dim and she could see that it was struggling as it made its way out of the box. The light flickered gently as Pandora's face began to reflect its glow. Pandora, through her tears and anguish asked, "What are you?" As the light strengthened and became beautifully bright, the white creature that had survived the depths of the darkness and pain inside the box simply said, "I am hope."

Hope is sometimes all we've got. When our clients convey a sense of hopelessness because their circumstances and their pain have become more of a burden than they believe they can bear, we can be there to remind them that even in the midst of the darkness, there is hope. I have often said to my clients in these difficult moments if they are feeling hopeless, no matter what, as their support person and their advocate, I am not feeling hopeless about their situation and so if they need to, even for a short time, they can borrow some of my hope until theirs returns. It is imperative we convey hope. Without hope, what do we have?

chapter six

What about My Pain?

"If you want others to be happy, practice compassion. If you want to be happy, practice compassion."

—DALAI LAMA

I had a class in graduate school that required us to write a paper about our personal "stuff." Specifically, we needed to write about our pain—the personal baggage we could potentially carry with us into our therapy sessions with clients and how we, as professional social workers, were going to handle this. The paper was an opportunity to begin the challenging experience of processing some of our life experiences and to examine how these experiences may affect our work with clients. My goal through the writing process was to examine my personal bias and how my clients' stories may, in fact, trigger emotional reactions in me because of my stuff.

The purpose of the class was to help future clinical social workers begin to look at the issue of transference and countertransference in the therapeutic relationship. Transference and countertransference are theoretically based in psychodynamic psychotherapy and loosely defined, as I understand it, when the client transfers perceptions, feelings, and beliefs onto the therapist based on the client's past experiences. Countertransference is what is elicited in the therapist during this process, that is, thoughts, feelings, and reactions to the clients' experiences that may be related to personal experiences. Understandably, this is why my graduate school professor found it incredibly important to begin the process of personal and professional self-exploration to emphasize the importance of awareness in relationships with clients. "What about my pain?" is a critically important question for social workers because, as human beings, we can easily be led down a path where our life experiences may enhance our work and benefit our clients' healing and recovery or, conversely, can harm our clients and place them at risk. This is an area that I find incredibly fascinating and of tremendous importance in our work. I do hope that professional social workers in all areas of the field spend time with peers, colleagues, and supervisors exploring these issues and assessing the nature in which they work with often highly vulnerable people who are counting on the professional to lead and guide them toward positive outcomes. If our personal baggage gets in the way of this, ethical disasters can and do occur.

Insight 1: Self-Disclosure

Our clients want to know us. They want to know and believe in our humanness and they want to have confidence in us and trust that we will understand their pain. This complex experience for the social worker can seem like a high-wire act, creating and executing the fine, purposeful steps that will ensure client safety while we embrace the role of helper. As our clients tell us their stories, we will inevitably be able to relate our own experiences to theirs. This will happen often and we need to be prepared about how we will handle ourselves, and in most cases, how we will cope.

A vivid recollection comes to mind as I think about the issue of self-disclosure. I have always known through my formal education and through the experiences outside the classroom through life education that when I am working with my clients, their needs come first. What this means in terms of self-disclosure is simple. If I decide to disclose information about myself or my experiences, then it must be to benefit the client. If I decide to disclose personal information and my motivation is because it will help me in some way or it will make me feel better, then I need to stop, immediately, and check myself. Client needs are our priority, always. What I vividly recall is an experience I had several years ago when I was meeting with the parents of a child who had died unexpectedly. They were struck with unspeakable grief. Their pain was all-consuming during our time together and I could literally feel it (transference–countertransference—aha!). Now this is where it can get tricky, because transference and countertransference are not something to necessarily be afraid of. This transfer of experience and emotion can actually be helpful and very useful in the therapeutic relationship.

I remember the mother of the child in particular because her pain was paralyzing her. She was not eating, sleeping, or functioning. The couple's grief was traumatic and had taken hold of every area of their lives. My work with them, as I saw it, was to assist in gently nudging them toward acceptance and healing. Our hope as social workers is that we can help our clients heal their pain through this sometimes-unimaginable process. As was the case with this couple, our goal was to be with one another and begin to figure out how to navigate through the pain—I truly believe the success in this case was the act of this couple bravely coming in for therapy and support. Their willingness to discuss something so privately painful and to examine this in therapy was amazing. As the therapist, had I pushed too hard for them to work on issues they were not ready to work on, it would have been disastrous for them. My sensitivity to their pain stemmed from my own pain and this is where in my experience, the process of using the countertransference process can be useful.

Before meeting with the grieving couple, I had a personal experience that I was able to draw from in terms of compassion and familiarity with the pain of loss. My brother and sister-in-law's child, their only son, had died unexpectedly and left our family in the depths of traumatic grief. The mind-numbing experience of the loss of a child is one that those who have experienced it will never forget. I witnessed my family's pain; I bore it with them and sometimes tried to bear it for them. As time has passed, I have been able to draw from that sad and painful place to help others. The wisdom I took from my family and their process has helped guide me in my work. In the case of grieving parents, I was able to listen, without fear or uncertainty, because I knew that I did not have the power to take their pain away. The pain of the loss was theirs and they would move through it as they were able. Unfortunately, we live in a "hurry up and get over it" society, and we are impatient when it comes to the necessity of time for grieving. Whether it is our own discomfort with others' pain, our need to feel in control in a very out-of-control experience, or simply our lack of understanding that leads to this kind of unrealistic expectation, we as social workers cannot buy into this belief system. Our clients will let us know how much time they need. We cannot and should not dictate this time frame, nor should we establish lofty expectations only to leave our clients feeling alone and frustrated in their pain. Grief may take a lifetime to overcome and hopefully there are moments of peace where the pain is less invasive and healing has taken place. It is an honor to be with people in the middle of this kind of emotional metamorphosis and one I draw from consistently in my work.

Insight 2: Practice What I Preach

Inherently, as social workers, our work is focused on giving. Frankly, we give until we can't give anymore and then, guess what? We give some more. We set ourselves up for stress, burnout, and medical and mental health problems if we do not recognize the importance of self-nurturance. I am certainly referring to the occasional massage, a date night with a friend or loved one, exercise, hobbies, and so forth. But I am also referring to the ongoing, daily practice of self-care, reenergizing, and renewing oneself to do the work of helping and to do it effectively without sacrificing our health in the process.

There are several steps I take each day to do a little spiritual, mental, and physical renewal. To illustrate this ongoing practice, I will share some insights into my typical workday with my interwoven self-care strategies highlighted. It is important to acknowledge that this is what works for me—it may not work for everyone. It has taken me most of my adult life to institute these steps. I frequently falter, forgetting myself in the midst of others' needs. It is always abundantly clear when I begin to slide in the area of self-care because I can feel it . . . in my body, my mind (my thoughts), and my spirit. All areas will suffer terribly if I do not stay aware and active with daily strategies. Here's what a positive, self-nurturing workday looks like for me:

- 5:15 a.m. My alarm goes off, I hit snooze, and my sweet little dog Stewart leaves his doggie bed and places his front paws on the side

of the bed, reaching up until I scoop him up for a short snuggle—
a GREAT way to start the day. (Insight: we all need unconditional
love and affection to do the work of compassionately caring for
others.)

- 5:22 a.m. My alarm goes off again. Stewie and I get up for the day,
wander to the coffeepot, pour a nice hot cup and head back to the
sofa for a little more snuggle time and contemplation about what
the day holds. (Insight: slow down and greet the day with a sense
of calm because the demands of the day are about to begin and
I may be better equipped to tackle them if I can carry a sense of
inner calm and well-being with me.)

- 5:30 a.m. I disengage Stewart from my lap and head to the floor
for some yoga and stretching. (Insight: it feels good to get my
blood flowing through deep, contemplative breathing and inter-
nalizing a sense of peace by clearing my mind's clutter about
future worries or "what ifs.")

- 6:00 a.m. I head back to the coffeepot for another cup, then
back to the sofa for some reading or meditation. A few selections
near me include *The Secret* (2006) by Rhonda Byrne, the bible,
and a variety of writings and drawings by Brian Andreas (2006).
(Insight: reading a brief and simple passage can set the tone for
the day and inspire me in the moment and frequently I will
draw from the inspiration all day long—whether purposefully or
subconsciously.)

- 6:20 a.m. I head to the shower, just after waking my kids and hop-
ing they decide to greet the day with some humor and gratitude.
(Insight: wake myself first and get ready for the day before I wake
others because it's amazing how my outlook influences others.)

- 7:30 a.m. I grab some sort of breakfast. I'm not much of a morning eater, but I know it's good self-care and I know I'll need the
sustenance so I usually try to find something remotely nourish-
ing. We head out the door. I pray. Sometimes I pray out loud or
sometimes it's silent prayer. I ask for patience, love, and guidance
for whatever the day holds. (Insight: we all need a little physical
and spiritual fuel to do the work we have set out to do.)

- 8:00 a.m. My work day begins. E-mails, followed by phone messages, followed by more phone calls, client sessions, supervisor requests, supervisor demands, crises, and perhaps a bathroom break. (Insight: it's important to prepare mentally, physically, and spiritually and to keep breathing; otherwise my work will reflect this and will be daunting versus fulfilling.)

- 12:00 p.m. I'd love to tell you I've taken a morning coffee break, but truthfully it doesn't happen. The place where I work is set in beautiful, natural surroundings. It's a historic place with a river running along its grounds, beautiful flowers in the spring and summer, and amazing fall colors in autumn: a great place to take a brisk walk and to breathe deeply for as long as I can. Walking on my lunch break is a priority. There are days I have to force myself to do it and have that back-and-forth argument in my head justifying why missing my walk just once wouldn't be such a bad thing. But I must go. I need to go. (Insight: take time to renew or my energy will dwindle long before it's time to go home and it will reflect in my work and with my clients—and my work identity is important but it's not my entire identity . . . there are many facets to *who* I am and all need to be cared for and honored.)

- 4:30 p.m. The workday begins to wind down and so do I. (Insight: whenever possible, I plan for the end of the day—I practice walking away from work, leaving nonpriority items for tomorrow because inevitably they will be there waiting for my attention and I'll be better equipped to address them in the morning.)

- 5:00 p.m. I pick up my children, my husband arrives home, and if I've thought of it, there is something taken out of the freezer for dinner. My commute home is brief and so I have taken necessary steps to officially switch gears when I walk into my house at the end of the workday. First, instead of starting dinner while talking to my kids, letting the dog out, and going through the mail simultaneously, I tell the kids to please let the dog out and leave the mail on the counter for later. I head to my closet to literally change roles for the night: work clothes and name badge off and comfy, mom, spouse, dog lover clothes on. And, I take my time. Once I became aware of the importance of the process of changing clothes, it made all the difference. (Insight: sometimes

it takes a concerted effort to change roles—leaving work at work can be difficult in our field and so finding a ritual that supports the transition of roles is an effective strategy.)
- 6:00 p.m. Dinner with my family. Preferably, we're sitting together at the table and engaged in conversation about our day's activities. If we can, we linger over the meal, empty plates, and conversation before we head off to our evening's activities. (Insight: talk to my family, connect with my children, and find things to discuss that have nothing to do with social work because it's healthy and necessary.)
- 9:00 p.m. Hopefully some reading (non-work-related books), time on the computer looking up recipes, connecting with friends by e-mail, or taking the dog for a short walk would be all of the ways I would prefer to end my day before climbing into bed getting ready to do it all over again the next day. (Insight: I need distractions—ways in which I tune out work and discover other things that energize and renew me.)

Self-care is a challenge for most of the social workers I know. We have a hard time focusing on ourselves, our needs, and our wants because we are programmed to be of service to others. To do the hard work we do, self-care is a must. Interestingly, when I've asked friends and colleagues in the field what they do for self-care, I'm frequently met with, "I know, I need to do more self-care" or "I'm not very good at self-care" or "Self-care, what's that?" From those who make valiant attempts at practicing self-care with any sort of regularity, I have gathered their suggestions, and perhaps their personal practices will inspire you to develop some of your own.

Self-Care Strategies from Social Workers in the Field
- Play with children—color, play with play dough, sidewalk chalk, jump ropes, Legos, swing on a swing, and so forth
- Sing your heart out to the radio either in the car or at home—move to the music, too!
- Build something with your hands
- Pay someone to have your house cleaned or barter the service

- Dig in the dirt
- Do some sort of craft—needlework, knitting, painting, scrap-booking, and so forth
- Read a book (not related to social work)
- Sleep late on purpose
- Get a massage
- Exercise
- Take a cooking class
- Yoga, meditation, or mindfulness practice
- Call a friend you haven't talked to in a while
- Take a nap
- Go to the movies
- Take a mental health day off from work
- Eat junk food for dinner
- Ask for a hug from someone close to you
- Go to a quiet place
- Stop talking for a couple of hours
- Look at old photo albums
- Lie in the sun
- Visit a place that's beautiful—a park, church, garden, and so forth
- Take a bubble bath with candles
- Join a club or organization
- Buy yourself flowers

We all need distractions. They're healthy and necessary to keep our energy level high and our stress level low. In our overscheduled world, we need to schedule time for self-care (as odd as it may seem). To be effective social workers, we need to prioritize the nurturance we give to ourselves every day. We tell our clients these same things, now we need to practice what we preach.

Insight 3: We're In This Together

I have a beautiful framed piece of artwork in my office by one of my favorite artists, Brian Andreas. It reads: "Someday, the light will shine like a sun through my skin and they will say, what have you done with your life? And though there are many moments I think I will remember, in the end I will be proud to say, I was one of us." I purchased the artwork when I got my first real job after completing graduate school. It was a celebration of "I finally made it!" The sentiment expresses what I believe is at the core of who I am as a social worker and human being. It guides my work life and my personal life and helps me to remember I am not alone and that no matter what, whether in the trenches of the social work field or in the trenches of life, there is an *us*.

I have the incredible opportunity to teach as an adjunct instructor at our local university and my undergraduate alma mater. It is joy to spend time with students who are finding their voices in terms of how they view the world and their valuable place in it. I learn a tremendous amount from students and from teaching. It keeps me inspired, learning, and in touch with others who like to ask lots of questions. The class I teach is about forming ideas about social issues, many of which are taken for granted by the general public but are at the heart and soul of what social workers do. The social justice element to the coursework keeps me cognizant of the greater world in which I live. Life is bigger than my job, my role, and my tiny corner on the earth.

I have also had the fortunate opportunity to provide licensure supervision to social workers in various work settings. When the supervision relationship is most effective is when the role encompasses that of student and teacher while frequently interchanging between the supervisee and me. What this means is that as I consult with professional social work peers about cases, conflicts, and successes, I am learning as much and some times more than the individual I am supervising. The process of supervising others in this capacity has encouraged me to continue my journey of discovery, professional self-assessment, and critical thinking skills. It is through this experience that I maintain my competence as a social worker in addition to the value of service in our work. I find the opportunity to "pay it forward" very rewarding in that I can help a fellow social worker move forward in their career. It's like the great metaphor of throwing a pebble in a pond and then watching the ripple effects on the water from the initial contact. If we as social workers have knowledge, experiences, and insight to share, why not share them in an effort to help someone else and enhance our profession as a whole? I am happy to report that there are many, many situations I have not encountered in my work, and the ability to learn from another in a mutually supportive and beneficial process has proven to be quite inspirational for me.

When I reflect on times in my professional life when I really needed to connect with others, graduate school comes to mind. There were moments when I was incredibly stressed out and questioning myself. Graduate education is rigorous and MSW programs are certainly no exception. I was working full-time and taking care of my family while attending night class, writing papers, and collaborating on group projects. Many of us have stories of survival and one of the things that helped me most was taking some time to see a therapist. I was not only interested in learning more about managing my own stress level but also wanted to do a kind of check-in regarding my readiness to be a clinical social worker. The therapist I found was a good sounding board, advocate, and teacher in terms of what I still needed to learn about myself to help others. Through this process, I was able to gain perspective about the work, my role, and the necessity of creating and implementing healthy practices in my life to avoid quickly becoming burned out. It is easy in our profession to suddenly realize that we see the world differently than others and that perhaps our perspective isn't always the healthiest. We work with people with problems—big problems. Because of the nature of our work, we may begin to see the world in a negative light if we're not careful and critically self-aware. Therapy can help. Therapy for me has created a balanced perspective about myself, other people, and the world around me. I want to continue to believe that people are intrinsically good and that we are all doing the best we can under the circumstances. It is when I slip away from this value that I know I need to talk to someone to get an objective and empathetic view of what might be occurring with me. My therapist, when I was somewhat critical of myself for needing help, said something I frequently repeat to my clients and that is, "Healthy people get help." Our work and our overall well-being depend on it.

chapter seven

Compassion Fatigue and Burnout

"Step with great care and great tact and remember that life's a Great Balancing Act."

—DR. SEUSS

On more than one occasion, I have heard myself utter aloud, "I can't listen to one more painful story." What follows in those moments of personal and professional stress is often a fantasy of what I would do if I wasn't in the social work field. What I tend to come up with is that I have no idea what I would do if I wasn't doing exactly the work I'm doing today. It is healthy to imagine a career outside the field. It is unhealthy to believe the field would be better off without me. It is the latter I need to avoid and so the importance of self-care and preventing professional burnout and compassion fatigue cannot be understated. It is when I experience the phenomenon with clients of "I can see your lips moving, but all I here is blah, blah, blah . . ." that I need to critically assess where I am emotionally, physically, and spiritually to preserve and protect myself and my clients. It is when we ignore these red flags that we place our clients and ourselves at risk. Much is written on professional burnout, compassion fatigue, and vicarious trauma within the helping profession. I have experienced all of the above and have included some of the warning signs I instinctively know will only lead me down a path I do not want to go. For me, compassion fatigue has looked like:

1. Feelings of hopelessness. I think of my job and my work life and wonder if I can do it effectively. I wonder if I'm any good to anyone. I wonder if anyone is able to get better or to find healing. I wonder if everyone in the world is in pain and it begins to overwhelm me.

2. Chronic feelings of dislike and discontent. I may even begin to despise the thought of going to work or I may look for reasons not to go in, perhaps excuses to stay home for the day and avoid people or situations that I am blaming for my own difficulties.

3. Personalizing. I begin to take client behavior personally or perhaps a co-worker or supervisor makes a comment that may be irrelevant to my work, but I find a way to make it about me.

4. Alienation. I may find myself in my office more frequently, isolated from co-workers and friends, for no apparent reason. Someone may invite me to lunch or to take a break and I find excuses to bury myself deeper in work.

5. Deriving limited enjoyment or satisfaction at work. I may find myself watching the clock, again looking for reasons to stay home or avoid others. I find little to get excited or passionate about or I may not find contentment in small successes, or, worse, I may not even notice them.

6. Dreams and nightmares. When my sleep is disturbed by client stories or work stressors and I have a difficult time shaking the dreams the following day I know I am experiencing some level of burnout. If I'm experiencing excessive insomnia, rumination, and worry about work, or I am preoccupied in my personal time with what's been left unfinished or perhaps I'm worrying about what clients are doing when I'm not with them, I know I'm struggling.

7. Tuning out. Some level of emotional insulation is incredibly useful when engaged in therapy with traumatized clients; however, emotional numbing is not conducive to the client-focused work I do. The numbing response has also occurred with co-workers and others in work settings, which leads to further isolation and discomfort.

8. Judgment. I may find myself engaged in hypercritical thoughts or comments to co-workers, family, and friends regarding my work.

I have difficulty finding anything positive to say and this plays out in my attitude and ability to overcome that overwhelming sense of hopelessness as outlined in number 1. As you can see, it can be a vicious cycle and can not only hurt me, but also can have devastating effects in my work.

As a therapist, I am a strong proponent for self-care; emotional, physical, and spiritual well-being; and keeping life in perspective and in balance. Do I consistently practice what I preach? Not always. Do I know the ways in which I can bring myself back into balance holistically? Absolutely. It's putting these practices in place that is often the greatest challenge. If we do not do this, however, we will suffer and our work will suffer. I've seen it occur over and over with friends, colleagues, and supervisors. The black hole becomes deep and overwhelming and the way out can be painful for the social worker who doesn't have the ability to critically self-assess and ask for help.

Of interest, for the first few years of my social work career, I believed that if I asked for help from co-workers or supervisors, they would perceive me as incapable or unable to effectively do my job. My professional fears and insecurities unfortunately led to a lot of unnecessary stress. The work we do is hard enough, we do not need to make it harder on ourselves by not asking for help when we need it.

While in my first year of child protection social work, I was working with an incredibly challenging parent who pushed many emotional triggers for me. The parent was angry. She was angry at the system, she was angry at her husband, the father of her children, and she was angry at herself. It wasn't until I accessed mutual support from my work peers and supervisor that I realized the anger, as personal as it felt, was not about me. The woman's husband had engaged in horrific abuse of their children and she was torn between her denial that her husband could have done what he did and her fear that the allegations could, in fact, be true, which meant in her mind she had failed as a mother. As the assigned social worker, it was my job to help keep the children safe and to assist the family in overcoming their devastating circumstances and attempt to heal some of the pain they had been experiencing long before I met them. But I, as an extension of the agency, was a target.

Over the months we worked together, the woman left aggressive and verbally abusive messages all hours of the day and night on my telephone voice mail. Her feelings toward the agency were intrusive and made our work together extremely challenging. There were moments when her rage about the injustices she perceived were occurring was unleashed on me. I could no longer take it. I had hit a wall, one of mental exhaustion and utter frustration. I would somehow find the strength to gently and firmly try to set limits, to redirect her verbal lashing out, assertively tell her to calm down, or I'd hang up the phone or shorten the face-to-face meeting we were having.

After weeks of continuous adversarial interactions, sleepless nights at home, feelings of inadequacy on my part, believing I was to blame for the woman's anger, I decided I had officially had enough. I talked to my husband the night before. I was scheduled to be at work. In my turmoil, with my husband's unwavering support, I walked into my supervisor's office the next morning and resigned my position with the agency. I gave up and I, at the time, believed it was in my best interest and the agency's best interest. After all, it was clear to me I didn't really know what I was doing and I didn't have the answers to "fix" my clients' problems. My supervisor was stunned as I handed her my letter of resignation. She said she had no idea that I had been struggling and she wondered why I hadn't come to her sooner with my concerns. I didn't have an answer for her. What occurred next is one of those "aha!" moments I hope everyone experiences many times throughout their careers. They are the tidbits of wisdom that come to us either from an individual with whom we can gain insight and wisdom or from an experience that changes the way we see ourselves and others. It's like the shift of the antenna on my grandparents' old TV set: the snowy static obscures our view, but with one slight movement in the right direction, the picture suddenly clears.

My supervisor said, "Sarah, stop trying to fix your clients." She shared her personal experiences of when she was a new social worker and took the time I needed that she didn't have, to give me insights into her struggles, which ultimately helped me with mine. It seems simple, doesn't it? If I share some of my pain and struggle with someone else, perhaps my pain and struggle can lessen. It is interesting to me after all this time how easy it is to forget that the very thing I ask my clients to do, I have at times been unable to do. It's being human, flawed, and far from perfect that gives me great relief and satisfaction in my work. It is not my job to fix my clients. It is my job as a social worker to help my clients find the tools to fix themselves. Wow, what a relief! My supervisor had been aware I was struggling and was waiting patiently for me to ask for help. I was able to admit because of her compassion and willingness to listen that I had been fearful of failure and of messing up my clients' lives, which led me to going it alone in the kind of work—child protection social work—that demands teamwork.

I kept my job for another year with the agency and eventually decided to move on and go back to graduate school. I took with me the invaluable lesson of letting others in on my struggle. Sharing my stress, consulting with those who may have creative ideas I had never even considered, and sometimes simply venting about frustrations are all imperative pieces to my survival in the field. I also embraced the fact that not all jobs in social work fit everyone. We all have individual strengths we bring to social work and through the sometimes painful professional learning process, we discover where we do and perhaps do not fit. The most important thing we need to remember is that burnout can harm our clients, damage our relationships, and hurt our profession. Self-care is necessary and self-awareness critical. We need to give ourselves and others permission to honestly look at where we are in terms of our own mental health and our work in the field. Being open and receptive to feedback from our co-workers, clients, supervisors, friends, and family is a key component to the work we love, social work.

Recommended Reading
(some of my favorites)

Andreas, Brian. (2006). *Some kind of ride.* Decorah, IA: Story People.

Bouris, Karen. (1996). *31 Words to create a guilt-free life: Finding the freedom to be your most powerful self. A simple guide to self-care, balance, and joy.* Makawao, Maui, HI: Inner Ocean.

Brown, Brené. (2007). *I thought it was just me (but it isn't): Telling the truth about perfectionism, inadequacy, and power.* New York: Gotham Books.

Figley, Charles R. (1995). *Compassion fatigue: Secondary traumatic stress disorders in those who treat the traumatized.* London: Brunner-Routledge.

Pipher, Mary. (2005). *Letters to a young therapist (art of mentoring).* New York: Basic Books.

Recommended Web sites (some of my favorites)

www.nasw.org
www.friedsocialworker.com
www.dailyom.com
www.compassionfatigue.org
www.socialworkerchat.org

Bibliography

Byrne, Rhonda. (2006). *The secret.* Hillsboro, OR: Beyond Words
Publishing.

Frankl, Viktor E. (1959). *Man's search for meaning.* Boston: Beacon.

Mitsakis, Aphrodite. (1996). *I can't get over it: A handbook for trauma
survivors.* (2nd ed.). Oakland, CA: New Harbinger.

National Association of Social Workers. (2006). *NASW code of ethics.*
Washington, DC: Author.

Radmacher, Mary Anne. (2008). *Live boldly.* Newburyport, MA:
Conari Press.

Index

Addiction
  treating, 17, 38
Avoidance
  as communication, 36

Career
  advocating for victims of sexual
    violence, 7
  as a new social worker, 2, 40–43
  child protection social worker, 2,
    10–12, 40–43, 58–60, 75–77
  chemical dependency treatment
    program, 17, 36–38
  chronological, 1
  facilitator, 22
  graduate school, 1, 42, 63, 72, 77
  licensure supervision, 71
  marital counseling, 5–6
  Minnesota, 10, 48
  outpatient mental health, 8, 26–29
  rape crisis center, 2, 23
  resignation, 76
  speaker on anger management, 46
  student and family advocate, 34–36
  teaching summer school, 14–16
  therapist, 5–6, 17–22, 36, 38,
    48–49, 75
  undergraduate school, 1, 39–40
  Veterans Affairs Medical Center,
    2, 42
  women's military sexual trauma
    group, 21–22

Client safety
  in social work, 44
  in therapy, 22, 26–29
Compassion fatigue
  checklist, 74–75
  in social work, 55, 73–75
Confidentiality
  in social work, 1
Coping skills
  teaching, 19–20
Cutting
  self-injury behavior, 24–26

Eger, Dr. Edith
  Holocaust survivor, 33
  motivational speaker, 33
  psychologist, 33

Feel Good File
  as part of career validation, 56
Frankl, Dr. Viktor
  author, 37–38
  founder of Logo Therapy,
    37–38
  Holocaust survivor, 37–38
  psychologist, 36–38

Healing
  as a goal, 21, 27–29, 32, 36, 38,
    58–60
Hope
  as a healer, 60–62